Uniting the Virtual Workforce

UNITING THE VIRTUAL WORKFORCE

Transforming Leadership and Innovation in the Globally Integrated Enterprise

KAREN SOBEL LOJESKI
RICHARD R. REILLY

WILEY

John Wiley & Sons, Inc.

This book is printed on acid-free paper. ∞

Copyright © 2008 by Karen Sobel Lojeski and Richard R. Reilly. All rights reserved.

Published by John Wiley & Sons, Inc., Hoboken, New Jersey.

Published simultaneously in Canada.

For general information on our other products and services, or technical support, please contact our Customer Care Department within the United States at 800-762-2974, outside the United States at 317-572-3993 or fax 317-572-4002.

Wiley also publishes its books in a variety of electronic formats. Some content that appears in print may not be available in electronic books.

For more information about Wiley products, visit our Web site at http://www.wiley.com.

Library of Congress Cataloging-in-Publication Data:

Sobel Lojeski, Karen
    Uniting the virtual workforce: transforming leadership and innovation in the globally integrated enterprise / Karen Sobel Lojeski, Richard R. Reilly.
        p.   cm. – (Microsoft executive leadership series)
    Includes index.
    ISBN 978-0-470-19395-2 (cloth)
    1. Virtual work teams–Management. 2. Communication–Technological innovations–Psychological aspects. 3. Alienation (Social psychology) 4. Employee motivation. 5. Organizational effectiveness. I. Reilly, Richard R. II. Title. III. Title: Leadership and innovation in the globally integrated enterprise.
    HD66.S648 2008
    658.4′022—dc22

                                                                        2007052397

Printed in the United States of America

10   9   8   7   6   5   4   3   2   1

Richard Reilly: In memory of Erik, the best person I ever knew.
and
Karen Sobel Lojeski: For my husband Paul whose invaluable help with this work made it possible, for my daughter Cezanne, and in memory of my Mother Maxine and Great Aunt Sally.

Microsoft Executive Leadership Series: Series Foreword

The Microsoft Executive Leadership Series provides leaders with inspiration and examples to consider when forming business strategies to stand the test of time. As the pace of change quickens and the influence of social demographics, the impact of educational reform, and the impetus of national interests evolve, organizations that understand and embrace these underlying forces can build strategy on solid ground. Increasingly, information technology is bridging social, educational, and international distances, and empowering people to perform at their fullest potential. Organizations that succeed in the enlightened use of technology will increasingly differentiate themselves in the marketplace for talent, raw materials, and customers.

I talk nearly every day to executives and policy makers grappling with issues like globalization, workforce evolution, and the impact of technology on people and processes. The idea for this series came from those conversations—we see it as a way to distill what we've learned as a company into actionable intelligence. Our authors bring *independent* perspectives, expertise, and experience. We hope their insights will spark dialogues within organizations, among communities, and between partners about the critical relationship between people and technology in the workplace of the future.

I hope you enjoy this title in the Microsoft Executive Leadership Series and find it useful as you plan for the expected and unexpected developments ahead for your organization. It's our privilege and our commitment to be part of that conversation.

Daniel W. Rasmus
General Editor, Microsoft Executive Leadership Series

Titles in the Executive Leadership Series:
Listening to the Future by Daniel W. Rasmus with Rob Salkowitz
Rules to Break and Laws to Follow by Don Peppers and Martha Rogers
Generation Blend by Rob Salkowitz
Uniting the Virtual Workforce by Karen Sobel Lojeski & Richard Reilly
Drive Business Performance by Bruno Aziza and Joey Fitts

Contents

Preface

In the past decade, virtual communications have provided tremendous gains for both individuals and organizations in the global workplace. Most professionals today are mobile—leveraging portable laptops and other devices along with anywhere anytime communications. This frees the 21st century worker from the confines of any given physical space or wall clock to work unfettered by space and time and able to access a vast array of knowledge and information. Flexible work arrangements have also made it possible for large numbers of otherwise disenfranchised people to participate more fully in the new millennium workforce. All this while, business productivity has risen dramatically.

Rarely, however, do we hear about any downsides or after-effects of virtual work, either in terms of added costs that actually deflate the bottom line or in the emerging mental health detriments resulting from the pressures of operating in a 24/7, "always-on" culture. For instance, one insurance company we worked with lost $3 million on one project alone due to issues surrounding virtual work. Employees were highly dissatisfied with their jobs and morale had all but bottomed out.

According to our research, these financial and social costs are accelerating and point to an emerging paradox: As communication technology advances increase, we feel more disconnected from work and each other than ever before. This produces a widening "gap" between rising productivity expectations and decreasing social well-being. And in this gap lives measurable and costly problems resulting from a growing sense of distance among the people caught in between. And we call it Virtual Distance.

Simply put, Virtual Distance is a psychological distance created between people by an over-reliance on electronic communications. As Virtual Distance rises, our data show that there are some staggering effects. Among them:

- 50% decline in project success (on-time, on-budget delivery)
- 90% drop in innovation effectiveness
- 80% plummet in work satisfaction
- 83% fall off in trust
- 65% decrease in role and goal clarity
- 50% decline in leader effectiveness

But can these losses be prevented? Is there a way to help each other feel more connected, to see ourselves as a meaningful part of an integrated organization and still take advantage of cost savings and productivity gains from virtual work? Can we control Virtual Distance to improve global team unity?

The answer to these and other questions is yes, if we begin to understand Virtual Distance—what it means, how to measure it, how to map it, and how to manage it.

For example, after we implemented various Virtual Distance mitigation techniques at the insurance company described above, project success rates increased substantially. Job satisfaction also improved. At a technology company in Silicon Valley, we're working with senior management to minimize Virtual Distance between the company and their

Gen-Y interns so they can attract and retain the best talent and, in turn, help young professionals feel more connected to the organization and aspire to a shared future.

After reading this book, we believe you'll agree that despite the "unbridled enthusiasm" for 24/7 work capabilities, forceful problems are affecting work in the Digital Age. However, by seeing these problems as the result of unregulated Virtual Distance, we can quantitatively understand how they're impacting the bottom line and disrupting the potential of teams and their individual members. Managing Virtual Distance, then, will provide a vivid road map for removing barriers to collaboration, innovation, and unity across the enterprise.

HOW THE BOOK IS ORGANIZED

Part One: Meeting, Measuring, Mapping, and Managing Virtual Distance

Chapter 1 gives a historical perspective on "distance," exposing the so-called "death of distance" as a myth and showing how our understanding of distance in the virtual workplace has to include not just physical spaces but the psychological gulfs that develop as we tap on our keyboards instead of each other's doors.

In Chapter 2 we make Virtual Distance visible by building and discussing the *Virtual Distance Model* and its three major parts: physical distance, operational distance, and affinity distance.

Chapter 3 shows the reader how Virtual Distance is measured, using the *Virtual Distance Index*, a tool we developed to quantify how Virtual Distance affects the most important aspects of work.

In Chapter 4 we "see" Virtual Distance through *Virtual Distance Mapping*, a powerful technique built to illuminate those flash points in a team structure, causing the most Virtual Distance.

Chapter 5 concludes Part One by describing how to manage Virtual Distance with specific tactics for overcoming both present and future Virtual Distance.

Part Two: High-Impact Virtual Distance Strategies

In Chapter 6 we focus on how virtual work has changed our understanding of how teams work and how Virtual Distance offers up a new universal language that transcends even the most culturally diverse and individualized team members.

Chapter 7 discusses the implications Virtual Distance has on *leadership* and why old-style leaders that do not adopt an *Ambassadorial Leadership* style, are ineffective in virtual workspaces.

Chapter 8 describes how *innovation* can be most damaged by Virtual Distance and provides crucial guidelines on how to avoid this important threat to continued growth.

In *Chapter 9* we look at the importance of selecting and using the right *technology* and *software* to help offset Virtual Distance.

And, finally, in *Chapter 10*, we discuss ways in which we can build a better and more connected future. We also share our concerns about how this could be derailed if the pace of technology expansion outruns our ability to reduce Virtual Distance and develop and maintain close human relationships in the virtual workforce.

Acknowledgments

We would like to acknowledge many people who have helped us in our ongoing work on Virtual Distance and related areas. Our sincere thanks to our Managing Editor at Microsoft, Daniel Rasmus. Dan was instrumental in helping us to establish a relationship with Wiley and helped us bring our ideas to life via this book. In addition, our Managing Editor at Wiley, Tim Burgard, was a constant source of help and support working with us whenever we needed him, helping us to shape this work, and coaching us on ways to best bring our concept to the general business audience. In addition, there were many friends and executives whom we collaborated with prior to and during our writing of the book. They include Charles House, the Honorable Jerry MacArthur Hultin, Karan Sorensen, Irving Wladawsky-Berger, Dr. Warren Axelrod, Sandy Lionetti and Alfred Bentley. We would also like to thank Dr. Martin Westwell for helping us to expand our thinking on how Virtual Distance affects our mental processes and brain functions. We thank all of our colleagues at Stevens Institute of Technology and the Institute for Innovation and Information Productivity. In addition, we thank those individuals who have supported our efforts over the long term including Dr. Edward Friedman, Dr. Alan Maltz, Anupam Gupta, Augie Campos-Marquetti, Roy Nicolosi, Vin Siegfried,

Rita Stringer, Dr. Edward Stohr, Dr. Niv Ahituv, Professor Bernie Skown, and Patrick McKenna. In addition, we thank some of our personal friends including Dr. Mary Jo Wilson, Ellen Pearlman, Heidi Bertels, and David Mogel Esq. Finally, we thank Mary Ellen Connell, Nick Pera, Ann Bamesberger, Ian Gover, Edel Keville, Guido Petit, Kevin Judge, Anthony Weicker, Michael LoBue, Peter Koen, Patty Leutchen, Janice Hutt, and Piet Hut with whom we have worked over past years and with whom we look forward to future collaborations. This book would not have been possible without these and hundreds of other people with whom we have talked, collaborated with, and who believe that people's well-being is the most important element in the virtual work equation.

Introduction: The Road to Virtual Distance

In 2002, anecdotal evidence was mounting that people were becoming increasingly dissatisfied with their work and employers. This news came at the same time that the most sophisticated and easily accessible communication tools, designed to increase collaboration all over the world, were being adopted. The widely accepted belief at this time was that information and communication technology (ICT) had unlimited benefits to corporations and individuals alike. It was well reported, for example, that information technology (IT) had accounted for a major increase in productivity. Between the years 1974–1995 labor productivity growth averaged 1.4 percent per year then rose to nearly 3 percent on average between 1995 and 2006.[1] Why, then, were individuals and teams struggling with significant communications problems and experiencing decreased satisfaction with work when, in theory, the opposite should have been true? This question began a journey that we continue to travel today. It led us to the discovery of Virtual Distance and its incredible impact on our work and personal lives.

The first step on this journey was to see what information we could find concerning virtual teams and related subjects, including "computer-mediated communications"

1

and dozens of other tangential topics. We found that there was very little research available on real-life workplace factors in global enterprises. Information about the worldwide organization and virtual work technology's effects on it, at least from a practitioner's point of view, was lacking.

So we decided we would do our own research. Over the course of our first year and a half of research, we conducted dozens of interviews with mostly three categories of people; C-level executives overseeing IT or business strategy; managers and individuals involved in virtual teamwork; and outsourcing managers. They came from a wide range of industries including financial services, pharmaceutical, management consulting, telecommunications, and consumer goods. We focused on three key questions:

1. *What did leaders consider virtual work?* This seemed a fundamental question since there was no common understanding of what virtual work actually meant and, therefore, no effective way to deal with related issues. For example, when we first started, we asked, "What do you consider to be virtual work?" Many equated virtual work with outsourcing. One manager said, "Well, for us, virtual work means that we have a lot of outsourcing relationships. And I can tell you that many of them are not working." But usually later in the conversations, the people we spoke with came to the conclusion that virtual workers included anyone connected to the company and to each other, by a laptop or other mobile computing device. As one manager put it, "I guess you could say that the entire company is made up of virtual workers, even though we have a policy that mandates everyone come into the office every morning. Many people 'talk' to each other using only IM [instant messaging] or e-mail, even if they physically sit in the office next door."

2. *How was management affected by working with virtual teams?* The answer to this question invariably reflected drastically increasing challenges. For example, one executive from a large financial services company told us, "I have thought about this a lot. I am not sure how to assess if I trust someone or not in a virtual environment. So I am constantly worrying about where my team is on any given project. I am trying to use old markers to evaluate virtual workers, and this does not work." Another manager from a major pharmaceutical company said that "since I don't have direct responsibility for some of the people I am managing, in addition to the fact that I rarely if ever meet them, it is very hard for me to give an accurate assessment of their performance. This is a huge challenge."

3. *What were the most salient organizational and strategic implications resulting from virtual work?* This question almost inevitably caused the interviewee to take a pause. One reason was that they realized that since virtual work was so prevalent, it was difficult to know where to start. Many thought that the issue of selecting the "right" business model was most difficult as typified by the response from a telecommunications executive, "Hierarchy becomes obsolescent in this environment. It used to be that you could delegate work down through the organization, and while this is still true to some degree, how do you coordinate and delegate to people that you do not have captive, those that work in virtual environments over whom you have very little control?" Another important issue was raised by the chief information officer at a major bank. He said, "Some of the technologies we use (to get the work done) are so esoteric that above a certain level in this organization, senior executives have no idea what we are doing. So you are

entirely on your own based on the principles that, in general, save the company money. In general, get the job done. In general, try to promote cooperation with colleagues. This is a global corporation with over 100,000 employees. We couldn't possibly understand what every person is doing."

Through these interviews, vivid patterns emerged around issues creating barriers to effective collaboration, communications, and trusting relationships in the virtual workplace. We categorized these findings into three groups: location-based issues like far-flung workers who never meet each other, day-to-day operational problems like too much multitasking and frequent miscommunications, and relationship-based challenges whereby people just weren't feeling as though they were connecting at a personal level.

When we stepped back and looked at all three areas, it became evident that each one represented a certain kind of distance. The issues related to location were clearly tied to physical distance. The daily trials and tribulations that constantly challenged people, like having to respond to too much e-mail and other distractions, created a psychological distance between co-workers. We called this operational distance. The last area we called affinity distance. Affinity distance stemmed from deep relationship divides caused by cultural disconnects and social issues that prevented people from getting closer to one another emotionally.

We realized that, when put together, all three issues combined to form a new phenomenon in the age of virtual work. We named this phenomenon Virtual Distance.

After we had named Virtual Distance, we wanted to find out to what extent it was interfering with collaboration on a larger scale. So we created an instrument, the Virtual Distance Index, to test for it. After three months, we had collected several hundred responses and, after analyzing the data, we found that indeed Virtual Distance existed

FIGURE 1 The Virtual Distance Formula

Virtual = Distance	Physical Distance +	Operational Distance +	Affinity Distance

across a wide spectrum of institutions among hundreds of project team members across dozens of different industries within various functions in the organization. We also found that Virtual Distance was just as likely to be found among collocated team members as between distributed workers. From these findings we were able to construct the Virtual Distance Formula shown in Figure 1.

Physical distance accounts for locational aspects, operational distance represents the many issues that disturb team members day to day, and affinity distance includes the myriad facets of fundamental relationship dysfunction across teams and organizations. In the research we conducted then, and in the many companies we work with today, we see that the majority of organizations are grappling with a combination of all three factors in varying degrees.

Once we had an idea about how far and wide this phenomenon had spread, we wanted to know the impact Virtual Distance was having on performance. So, in addition to collecting data on the Virtual Distance Index itself, we asked about other factors like the ability to deliver projects on time and on budget, and whether innovation problems were arising. From these answers we could see that Virtual Distance was having a major impact. Statistically, the correlations were very strong between high Virtual Distance and fall-offs in financial success and innovation. We discovered that trust, clarity around roles and goals, and people's willingness to help one another all suffered tremendously as Virtual Distance grew, and it was through these dynamics that corporations were feeling the financial sting and innovation pain of Virtual Distance.

Since we began our research, there have been growing signs that work satisfaction continues to decline. According to a recent study done by The Conference Board, less than half of the American workforce is satisfied with their jobs, representing a 61% decline over the past two decades.[2] And we now know that Virtual Distance is one of the major contributing factors to this troubling trend.

It is our hope that this book will engender a better understanding of Virtual Distance and the impact it has on people and performance in today's workplace, and then provide some tools for minimizing its impact going forward. We begin with a look back and discuss how and why distance has always played a major role in organizational history and why it needs to be redefined in the Digital Age.

NOTES

1. The Congressional Budget Office, *Labor Productivity: Developments since 1995*, www.cbo.com.

2. The Conference Board, *U.S. Job Satisfaction Declines, The Conference Board Reports*, www.conference-board.org.

Part One

MEETING, MEASURING, MAPPING, AND MANAGING VIRTUAL DISTANCE

~ 1 ~

Redefining Distance

Imagine a time traveler from the 1960s instantly transported to 2008. They would see some truly astonishing things going on: people working and collaborating across cities, time zones, and even continents; messages sent to anyone, anywhere, anytime without using the U.S. mail; other people attending meetings virtually from their offices, hotels, or even homes; and the ability to easily keep in touch with coworkers in the oddest places like air terminals, trains, cars, and golf courses. The world of work in the twenty-first century is a very different place than it was 40 years ago, and we don't just mean dressing business casual.

It is technology, of course, that has made all of this possible. Nobody, not even the best science fiction writers, envisioned how the way that we work would change or how rapidly the changes would occur. In some respects, it may seem that we have eliminated distance as an impediment to working effectively. After all, we can instant message our colleague in China while we're both looking at the same PowerPoint slides. Or, even better, we can have face-to-face contact using new high-definition videoconferencing.

But any funeral plans for the "death of distance" are premature. While our technology allows us to communicate in amazing new ways, distance is still an important issue. Most people think of distance as geographic separation, but it turns out that geographic separation is only part of the distance equation. Distance can have several meanings. It can refer to separation in time, separation between two points in space, or emotional separation. Our research with virtual teams began with the notion that geographic separation created emotional distance between coworkers. We quickly realized, however, that geographic separation was only one and not even the most important element in creating a sense of distance. We coined the term *Virtual Distance* to refer to the psychological distance that results when people interact mainly through electronic media—no matter where those communications originate and end. Virtual Distance can vary depending on many factors, real as well as perceived. We will discuss these in detail in Chapter 2, but first, let's consider why the "death of distance" myth creates a slippery slope that is at best woolly when it comes to understanding human behavior.

LOCATION, LOCATION, LOCATION

In the 1970s, Thomas Allen, a researcher at Massachusetts Institute of Technology (MIT), conducted a study on communication patterns. He visited seven different research-and-development laboratories and asked scientists and engineers to indicate the people they communicated with and how frequently they communicated. Allen then measured the distance between the desks of all of the people in each organization. He found that the probability of communicating with someone became lower as the distance between the desks became higher. Discovering this linear relationship was hardly surprising; what was surprising was that distance mattered only for the first 30 meters. After that, the probability of communication fell to almost zero. This relationship held even after Allen corrected for organizational factors such as group and disciplinary affiliation. In short, if your coworker was in another building, he might as well have been 3,000 miles away.[1]

Of course, you are probably thinking that Allen's work was done before the Internet existed. But as those of us who were working in the 1970s remember, we did have a device called the telephone. So what Allen found cannot be entirely explained away by information and communication technology (ICT), like that used for the Internet, e-mail, instant messaging (IM), or SecondLife and other virtual worlds.

Let's consider a more recent study that looked at how the effects of "perceived distance" influenced the interactions between two people. The first study randomly assigned people to one of two conditions. In the first condition, people were told that they were communicating with a partner who was a few miles away, in the same city. In the second condition, people were told that the partner was in a city 3,000 miles away. The results showed that the perception of distance had a significant effect on the subjects. When subjects thought their partner was far away, they were less likely to cooperate with them, more likely to deceive them, and less likely to be persuaded by them. This was true whether the interaction was via IM or videoconferencing. In reality, the partner was in the next room, so it was simply the cognitive interpretation or feeling of distance that produced these results.[2] So much for technology bringing about the "death of distance"!

Physical or geographic separation is clearly an important factor in the kinds of relationship that we develop with others. But why does *thinking* that someone is far away change our behavior? One reason is that we expect future interactions and especially face-to-face meetings to be unlikely if someone is 3,000 miles away. If we behave in a disagreeable way, we're not likely to be confronted in person. Therefore, there is less consequence and meaning ascribed to interactions that are not physically near.

A second reason is emotional sensitivity. Consider the following scenario: Imagine you're in a control room monitoring rail traffic. The computerized system allows you to view obstacles on the tracks and to control switches. In a location 100 miles away, you see that one of the trains is approaching the left side of a fork in the track at top speed. On the left side, five rail workers are fixing the track. On the right side, there is only one worker. You must decide whether to switch the train to the right side or leave the train heading toward the five workers.

This is a rather unpleasant moral dilemma, but research shows that most people would throw the switch and save five lives at the cost of one. But now consider a modified version of the scenario: Imagine that you are on a bridge watching a train hurtling toward five workers just over a ridge. If the train doesn't stop, the workers are sure to die. You happen to notice a large man standing precariously on the bridge watching the train. If you sneak up on him, and push him off the bridge, he will fall to his death onto the track. But, because he is so big, he will stop the train. You must decide whether to push him over or allow the five workers to die.

This second dilemma is even more unpleasant, but the consequences of the choices are identical. In this case, research shows that few people would choose to push the big man to his death, even though it would save five lives.

Modified versions of these two scenarios[3] have been used to study moral and ethical behavior. In an attempt to understand why people react so differently to these two scenarios, researchers at Princeton University used magnetic resonance imaging (MRI) scans to show that the first scenario activated areas of the brain typically involved in making logical, impersonal decisions, such as choosing a route for a trip. But the second scenario activated an entirely different area of the brain—one that is activated when strong emotions are involved.

We believe that Virtual Distance creates similar differences in the emotional reactions of individuals working together. When Virtual Distance is low, the emotional ties with coworkers are stronger. Low Virtual Distance also means that people are more likely to trust their coworkers and feel committed and motivated to the mission. As we shall see, this doesn't necessarily mean that people need to be collocated in order to reach a state of low Virtual Distance. In fact, some of our data show that two people working in the same building can have high Virtual Distance between them. The greater the Virtual Distance among the members of a team, the more problems—miscommunication, lack of clearly defined roles, even personal and cultural conflicts—the team will experience.

VIRTUAL DISTANCE THOUGHT EXPERIMENT

Think of a friend you have known for a long time but haven't seen in a while because she lives far away. When you do speak with her on the phone or read an e-mail from her, it is as if you just saw her yesterday and are simply picking up where you left off.

That's an example of Low Virtual Distance when geographic separation is high.

Now think of someone you work with, perhaps someone in the same office a couple of cubicles or offices away. You rarely talk to her, and when she needs to talk to you, she sends you an e-mail rather than walking over to your desk. When you are face to face, you can't help feeling a bit uncomfortable—after all, most of your communications have taken place through the computer, and you don't know each other at all.

That's an example of high Virtual Distance when geographic separation is low.

The Virtual Distance thought experiment underscores another important point: Virtual Distance is a phenomenon that has an influence on everyone who uses ICT to communicate on a regular basis—in business as well as personal affairs. In organizations in particular, Virtual Distance is a state that can have an effect on the entire enterprise ecosystem, from the boardroom to the bench, from customer service to the company's customer's customer. While there are such things as "virtual teams," which are usually described as a group of people who are geographically separated, sometimes culturally different, and who use a lot of virtual communications, they are not the only subset of corporate resources that could benefit from overcoming Virtual Distance.

Some of us remember the days when most of our interactions were with people in the same building, e-mail did not exist, there was no fax, no voice mail, and most of our communications were synchronous. The U.S. Postal Service still handled a lot of our communications, and we still could use the excuse that the report was "in the mail."

Of course, all of that has changed, and the changes have come about quickly. E-mail, for example, has been around only about 20 years, mobile phones and handheld devices such as Blackberries only 10 years. At the same time, other changes have been taking place. Increased globalization; increased cultural, organizational, and national diversity; a movement from hierarchical to networked organizational structures; and ever-increasing connectedness are occurring simultaneously.

GLOBALIZATION, DIVERSITY, AND NETWORKS

Here's a description of a company that might sound familiar. It has widely dispersed teams of managers who rarely see one another face to face and communicate mostly asynchronously. They outsource critical parts of their business to individuals whose language, culture, and values are quite different. This is a pretty good description of most global businesses today, but we're describing a company that began in Great Britain over 300 years ago.

The Hudson's Bay Company is best known today for its Canadian Department Stores, but in the 1700s and 1800s, Hudson's Bay was the premier fur-trading business in the world.[4] Managers were located in widely distant outposts throughout North America and, because of the distance and geographic dispersion, were given fairly wide latitude and discretion in decision making—an example of what we might term today as *empowerment.*

Outsourcing was also important for Hudson's Bay. All of the furs came from trappers who were Native American peoples in what is now the Northern United States and Canada. Although they didn't have Blackberries, Hudson's Bay employees faced many of the same challenges facing today's managers. Geographic distance, cultural differences, asynchronous communication, coordination, and interdependence of tasks were issues that affected the Virtual Distance between the Hudson's Bay managers.

The example of Hudson's Bay shows that globalization is not a new phenomenon. The Roman Empire was a global institution, or at least for the part of the globe that was known at the time. For centuries, the Empire was able to manage geographically dispersed and culturally distinct social and economic groups quite effectively. The Silk Road during the Mongol Empire is another example. What is new is the pace and pervasiveness of globalization over the past several decades.

Researchers at the Konjunkturforschungsstelle Swiss Institute for Business Cycle Research in Zurich have been carefully tracking the growth of globalization since 1970. They devised an index that combines economic, political, and social indices of globalization into one

Development of globalization across the world

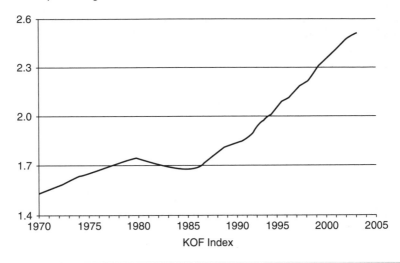

FIGURE 1.1 Growth of Globalization

Konjunkturforschungsstelle index of globalization, which they (thankfully) call the KOF Index. Economic factors include long-distance flows of goods, capital, and services as well as information and perceptions that accompany market exchanges. The social dimension measures the spread of ideas, information, images, and people, while the political dimension captures diffusion of government policies. Figure 1.1 shows the rapid and steady growth of globalization worldwide since 1970.

Technology is clearly one of the most important factors in increased globalization. We can be thousands of miles apart, and we can easily transfer large amounts of data at high speeds, engage in relatively clear communication, and even work on the same document at the same time. But while some things are easy across great distances, other things may not be that easy. We might have to build relationships and work with outsourcers, team members, and employees whom we have never met (and may never meet) face to face.

Working across international boundaries carries additional complications. Coworkers may be from very different cultures, with different values, communication styles, beliefs, and attitudes. This increase in diversity has some benefits. Understanding local cultures may be important if we're planning to launch a new product, for example, and the different knowledge, skills, and ways of thinking inherent in multicultural teams can be an advantage in developing new approaches to solving business problems. But the same cultural differences can create misunderstanding and conflict.

Consider the following situation between French and American employees working on the same team. The French view information as centrally controlled by a hierarchically managed bureaucracy, which in this case is different from the American belief that information can be shared within empowered and autonomous teams. The French people placed a high level of importance on building long-term relationships with customers, whereas the same was discounted by Americans who viewed this as an impediment to good business practice.[5]

French beliefs notwithstanding, the movement toward flat, decentralized organizational structures has increased over the past decade. Decentralization has some great benefits. Because employees and teams are empowered, they can make decisions more quickly. And speed can be critical for getting new products out, where first to market can be a big competitive advantage.

But decentralization also means that the way we communicate has changed. Instead of having to go through a chain of command, communication can be more direct between people, teams, and organizational units. It also means that informal networked structures have become even more important than they used to be. Networked structures more appropriately describe the relationship between multinational organizational units and their suppliers, for example, but also describe the relationship between people working in those structures. Social Network Analysis (SNA) offers a useful set of tools for describing the relationships between organizations, subunits and individuals within these net-worked organizations. As we will discuss later, many SNA concepts have direct implications for Virtual Distance.

THE YIN AND YANG OF WORK

Antonio Damasio is a neuroscientist who has studied how our brains function when we make decisions.[6] Case studies of brain injuries led Damasio to an interesting conclusion. When we make decisions, our brains do two things: con-duct an analysis of the situation and alternatives involved in the decision, and conduct an emotional evaluation of the situation and the options. It turns out that if the connection between the emotional center and the analytic center is in-terrupted, we can't make a decision. We might be able to conduct a thorough analysis of all of the pros and cons, but without the emotional connection, we simply can't choose.

What does brain functioning have to do with the way we work? Work is nothing more than a series of decisions. Some of these may be highly programmed and may not in-volve much thought. But most of the more interesting work that we do involves using our brains—both the analytical and the emotional sides—to make decisions. The Chinese concept of yin and yang, used to describe two opposite but complementary forces, nicely describes this dichotomy. Many managers tend to be great at the analysis side, but not so great at connecting to the emotional side of the employ-ees who are doing the work. This dichotomy appeared and reappeared in different guises during the twentieth century in the ideas and theories of social scientists who study work behavior.

One of the most important examples of this dichotomy is the difference between Frederick Winslow Taylor and

Elton Mayo. In 1911, Taylor published *Scientific Management*,[7] which laid out a new approach to making work more efficient by designing tools and the procedures that could optimize work efficiency. Taylor's view was that the worker using the tools was a rather inefficient, but unfortunately necessary, component of production. His views of the average worker were expressed in his testimony before congress in 1913: "I can say, without the slightest hesitation, that the science of handling pig-iron is so great that the man who is . . . physically able to handle pig-iron and is sufficiently phlegmatic and stupid to choose this for his occupation is rarely able to comprehend the science of handling pig-iron."[8]

Taylor was a mechanical engineer. He invented the field of industrial engineering. Engineers are generally trained to approach problems analytically and find technology-based solutions. While this approach has led to many important advances, it has also persistently ignored the attitudes, values, and emotions of the human beings actually performing the work. In fact, the persistence of this phenomenon was remarkable throughout the twentieth century, even influencing our current work environments.

Of course, Taylor was not alone in his view of the worker. In the 1890s when Taylor started his studies, the standard workweek was about 60 hours over six days,[9] with no health insurance, pension plans, or overtime. Concerns about the "feelings" of workers were not exactly a priority. But in the 1920s, this bleak view of the worker as another machine began to change.

The signal event actually began as another effort at "Taylorism." Industrial engineers at the Western Electric Company were interested in finding the optimal level of illumination for production workers. They conducted the first few studies at the Hawthorne Works in Cicero, Illinois, in the 1920s. They selected a group of workers and increased the illumination or lighting in the room. Productivity went up as a result. They increased it some more, and productivity went up again. They then decreased the illumination, and productivity went up even more. Obviously, something more than illumination was causing the changes in productivity. A consultant, Elton Mayo, was brought in to help figure out what was happening.

After looking at the results of the illumination studies, interviewing the workers, and conducting his own research, Mayo concluded that there was an entirely different set of factors involved in the increases in productivity. He found that the interest and sympathy of the supervisor and the attention paid to the workers had impacts on motivation, for example. He also found that when workers were given a bit of autonomy, they were able to see themselves as a team, which increased a sense of control and increased their commitment to the work. Mayo's conclusions may seem rather obvious today, but in the 1920s these views were radical—so radical that U.S. business and industry pretty much ignored the findings.[10]

The distinctness between analytical tasks and emotional behavior continued. In 1950, for example, a series of research studies at Ohio State University concluded that the two major factors that distinguished the performance of leaders were initiating structure and consideration. *Initiating structure* is a shorthand term for analysis, planning, and problem solving; in other words the analytical side of work. *Consideration* refers to the leaders' concern for the social and interpersonal side, that is, the emotional side. The Managerial Grid that emerged in the 1960s used a similar concept and rated leaders on concern for productivity and concern for people. Figure 1.2 shows that these two factors emerge consistently in research on leadership, trust, prediction of work performance, job satisfaction, and project performance.

FIGURE 1.2 The Yin and Yang of Organizational Theories

Theory or Research	Analytical (Yin)	Emotional (Yang)
Ohio State Leadership Studies (1950s)	Initiating structure: planning, organizing, problem solving	Consideration: Leaders must consider the social and interpersonal needs of followers
Theory X and Theory Y (1960s)	The manager's job is to structure the work and energize the employee	People are self-motivated by the satisfaction of doing a good job
Managerial Grid (1964)	Concern for production	Concern for people
Full Range Leadership Theory (1980s)	Transactional leadership	Transformational leadership
Project Management Research (1990s–2000)	Budgets, schedules, and milestones	Project spirit, leadership, and behavior
Theories of interpersonal trust (1990s)	Cognitive trust—trust based on rational expectations	Affective trust—trust based on relationships
Prediction of work performance (employee selection research)	Cognitive ability	Personality and emotional/social intelligence
Job satisfaction	Satisfaction derived from work content	Satisfaction derived from peers

VIRTUAL WORK AND VIRTUAL DISTANCE

As we have seen, geographic distribution and globalization of work are not entirely new phenomena, but the Internet, broadband, and other technology, allow us to communicate and work together in ways that were not possible before their combined arrival.

Working virtually creates new challenges for communication, leadership, and teamwork, and like Frederick Taylor, modern managers seek solutions by designing better tools. In this case, the tools might be collaborative design software, high-speed video, or a better conferencing system. But, also like Taylor, most see technology as the solution when it may just be creating another problem.

Our research and experience in consulting with diverse organizations has led us to the conclusion that improving the effectiveness of the virtual workforce does not lie in better technology. As Chuck House, the director of Stanford's Media X lab, says, "The more virtual distance, the less sophisticated the software should be."

So how does a company go about understanding whether Virtual Distance is an issue within their organization? The first thing they need to do is to meet Virtual Distance. This provides an important structure that allows a basis for effectively tackling the myriad and complex issues that arise in virtual teams. The next chapter introduces the reader to the details of the Virtual Distance Model and provides the scaffolding for dealing with its challenges.

SUMMARY

1. The "death of distance" is a myth. The truth is that we continue to grapple with distance-related

problems based on geographic separation as well as emotional separation—just as we have for centuries.

2. Physical distance can create barriers to communication even with technology-enhanced collaboration tools. Here are just a few examples:

    • 30 meters was found to be the physical limit for face-to-face communications in the mid–1950s, when telephones were available to bridge geographic distance.

    • Half a century later, in 2004, studies found that people cooperate less, deceive more, and are less persuaded when just the "perception" of physical distance increases.

    • Ethical choices and emotional attachment are both heavily influenced by physical closeness.

3. Globalization of work and outsourcing are not new concepts, but the extensive use of high-speed information and communication technology have made distance issues more acute in the twenty-first century than ever before—a critical driver for renewing our understanding of how distance plays a role in the context of our new world of work.

4. Emotional as well as analytical or task-related considerations have been competing for space in management theories since the dawn of management science itself. Perceived distance brought on by ubiquitous technologies has a profound and measurable effect on both.

5. *Virtual Distance* is a new term we have coined to describe the distance-related factors that affect us most in the Digital Age. These include, not surprisingly, a combination of geographic as well as social and emotional distances and feelings of separation, which can inhibit collaboration, communication, and success.

NOTES

1. T. J. Allen, *Managing the Flow of Technology* (Cambridge, MA: MIT Press, 1977).

2. Erin Bradner and Gloria Mark, Why distance matters: Effects on cooperation, persuasion and deception, *Proceedings of Computer Supported Cooperative Work* (November, 2002, New Orleans, LA), 226–235.

3. Carl Zimmer, Whose life would you save? *Discover,* (2004): 60–65.

4. Michael B. O'Leary, Geographic Dispersion in Teams: Its History, Experience, Measurement, and Change, (Doctoral Diss., Massachusetts Institute of Technology, 2002).

5. Marietta L. Baba, et al. The contexts of knowing: Natural history of a globally distributed team. *Journal of Organizational Behavior,* 25 (2004): 547–587.

6. Antonio R. Damasio, *Descartes' Error: Emotion, Reason, and the Human Brain* (New York: Harper Perennial, 1995).

7. F.W. Taylor, *Scientific Management* (New York: Harper & Row, 1911).

8. R. Kanigel. *The One Best Way: Frederick Taylor and the Enigma of Efficiency* (New York: Penguin Books, 1997).

9. Thomas J. Kniesner, The full-time work week in the United States, 1900–1970, *Industrial and Labor Relations Review,* 30 (1976): 3–15.

10. E. Mayo, *The Human Problems of an Industrial Civilization* (New York: MacMillan, 1933).

~ 2 ~

Meeting Virtual Distance

In Chapter 1, we talked about distance and the major role it plays. As we discussed, Virtual Distance can impede effective collaboration in the Digital Age. Virtual Distance can be described as a feeling—a sense one gets of being psychologically far away from others. It's different than other kinds of distance in that it has qualities that are derived from both real distance, like physical separation, and perceived spaces that develop from social gaps, as well as day-to-day attempts to balance enormous amounts of work with building meaningful relationships.

As we will see later on, Virtual Distance can cause havoc with financial results, innovation as well as other important aspects of work. But first it's important to understand what contributes to this sense of separation among us. This chapter introduces you to specific facets of Virtual Distance and provides a foundation on which solutions can be developed to increase performance, improve trust, enhance innovation, and get better bottom-line results from the virtual workforce.

CASE STUDY

The chief information officer (CIO) of a large international bank had been struggling for many years to understand what was working and what wasn't among his virtual workforce. During that time, he'd developed a large pool of virtual workers including in-house staff housed in distributed and sometimes remote locations throughout the world as well as low-cost development resources from outsourcing companies throughout India and China. During our interview with him, he shared an approach he was using to get a grip on virtual workforce obstacles. He'd tracked and collected data on over 50 project criteria for three years, hoping to pinpoint patterns that would lead to virtual team improvements. His methodology was quite innovative. However, after 36 months, much to his dismay, it revealed little about why projects succeeded or failed. We spent some time showing him how the Virtual Distance Model could be used to more accurately and quickly uncover the problems which were at the root of his concerns about project success.

Virtual Distance is an easy concept to grab hold of at first. Everyone has some direct experience with either low Virtual Distance or high Virtual Distance. The thought experiment in Chapter 1 revealed one way to get to know Virtual Distance. But Virtual Distance has an underlying and identifiable structure that's important to understand. It is this structure that allows us to directly measure it. It's like the "dynamics DNA" of the virtual workforce. So let's take some time to walk through the Virtual Distance Model to better understand the forces at work that make us "feel" far apart.

Virtual Distance contains three major pieces:

1. *Physical distance*—those factors that are based on real location differences in both space and time

FIGURE 2.1 The Virtual Distance Formula

Virtual = Distance	Physical Distance +	Operational Distance +	Affinity Distance

2. *Operational distance*—psychological gaps that grow due to the many day-to-day problems that arise in the workplace

3. *Affinity distance*—the emotional disconnects between virtual team members rooted in a lack of fundamental relationship development

These three parts are represented in the Virtual Distance Formula which we introduced in Chapter 1 but show again here in Figure 2.1.

PHYSICAL DISTANCE

Physical distance (see Figure 2.2) represents the many varied ways in which we're separated by real things including geography, time zones, and organizational affiliation. As

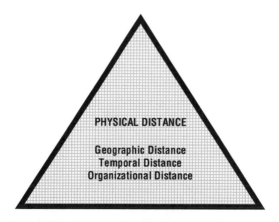

FIGURE 2.2 Physical Distance

we discussed in Chapter 1, globalization has dramatically altered the extent to which these kinds of distances exist between us.

According to a recent Stanford University study, one out of every five professionals has never met their boss.[1] Imagine, 20 percent of the workforce begins each day with basically no idea about who they report to aside from the occasional phone call, maybe a bio and picture on a web site, and a lot of e-mails. What's even more astonishing, according to the same research, is that over half of those that have never met their managers, don't think they'll *ever* meet. So they start each day without any expectation that they'll ever see their boss in person.

This lack of an anticipated future encounter may produce behaviors that are not what the leadership wants. For example, one of the most difficult things to do is to say "no" to a manager, ask for a raise, or to bring a problem to the table under any circumstances. And it becomes even more difficult if there's no prospect of ever meeting them. So leaders that expect issues to be raised and made visible by far-flung resources are indeed facing a kind of blindness instead because, in many instances, those they expect to point out problems are not likely to do so.

Some think that being virtual makes it easier for people to speak their minds.[2] But this can also be highly misleading and even detrimental to work. According to Bradner and Mark (Chapter 1), just the "perception" of distance causes dysfunctional behaviors like deception and less cooperation.

So if many believe that they might never or at best rarely see their manager, and also have a hard time saying "no" or pushing back in any way, then it's no surprise that physical distance gets in the way of problem solving, innovation, and other critical outcomes in the global world.

There are three components of physical distance included in the Virtual Distance Model:

1. Geographic distance
2. Temporal distance
3. Organizational distance

Geographic Distance

Geographic distance is simply what it says—the distances between us that can be measured using inches, feet, miles, and so on. Geographic distance is the factor which gets the most attention among managers and virtual team leaders. But it turns out that geographic distance is neither necessary nor sufficient to create Virtual Distance. But when it is at issue, it's a "fixed" condition, challenging us in many important ways, including finding methods that help us develop and maintain effective communications.

It's tricky because when we're geographically distant, our innate social skills are unavailable. For example, when someone we're talking with face to face doesn't look us in the eye, we suspect they may be hiding something. This inherent suspicion, which is usually quite accurate, results from our "normal" communication mode when we derive understanding through visual cues like facial expressions and body language. But when we can't see them, it's not possible for us to use the senses we're born with to decode someone's intentions or sincerity. And when we can't accurately decipher others' behaviors, we don't react naturally or even appropriately.

A lack of physical proximity makes us all a bit uncomfortable. For example, a high-ranking military official who had used virtual teams to implement a major organizational transformation said, "Virtual presence is actual absence." After having worked with people he wasn't close to, he'd grown pessimistic about the value of such a workforce compliment.

However, in our original research as well as our current consulting practice, we've encountered many people who feel that meeting just once, or at critical times, can help minimize the effects of geographic gaps. One research participant said, "While working face to face is the best, relations with distant-location people can build up over time. The key to relationship building is to build up trust between the parties. I find that even one meeting face to face can be an enormous help to establishing a good rapport with others."

In summary, geographic distance contributes to a sense of being far away because, in fact, one *is* far away. So we cannot expect that people will be able to work through communication problems the way they would if they were face-to-face. And in today's modern workplace, it's often impossible or even undesirable to get together some, if not most, of the time. But, as we'll see a bit later, the effects of geographic separation can be overcome by fixing problems in the other aspects of Virtual Distance.

Temporal Distance

Temporal distance is the separation caused by time zone differences as well as disparities in work schedules. The most significant issue that arises from time-related problems is coordinating work. Getting tasks into the right sequence and developing a steady rhythm among virtual team members is important to producing high-quality performance. But temporal distance wreaks havoc with this effort.

For example, if one person is located on the East Coast of the United States and another is working in Beijing, China, the time difference between them is at a maximum because they are literally 13 hours apart. One person is probably sleeping while the other is working—under "normal" circumstances, that is. We say this because sometimes, to

overcome time zone differences, managers schedule meetings that occur in the middle of the night for some. While
working this way might help to solve problems in the short
term, over the long haul, regularly scheduling meetings that
upset people's normal paces (body clocks, etc.) can weaken
team relations and have a negative impact on performance
and innovation.

For example, at a large financial services company, software application development was done using resources
separated by multiple time zones. There were people based
in New York, South America, eastern Europe, India, and
China. When one had questions for the other, they'd communicate via e-mail and then have to wait 24 hours for a
response. Productivity suffered and frustration soared, especially under tight deadlines. Days and sometimes a week or
more could pass before a single issue was resolved satisfac-
torily. Project momentum faded, and it was delivered late
and over budget.

In summary, temporal distance specifically contributes
to the sense that we're not well coordinated and can't establish any kind of predictable or regular rhythm. Therefore,
solving temporal distance requires managers to establish re-
liable assurance about when things are going to happen,
where, and so forth. Only then can those who feel far away
based on time displacements begin to experience more
closeness by anticipating work schedules that prove to be
dependable.

Organizational Distance

Organizational distance is a sense of separateness brought
on by differences in organizational affiliations. For example, Joe and Ramesh need to work together. Joe works
for Acme Consumer Goods and Ramesh works for ABC
Outsourcing. At a major chemical company, Jack and Jill

are also required to work together. But Jill works in New Product Development and Jack works for the Supply Chain Management Division. Sometimes Jack and Jill need to talk to Joe and Ramesh because they're all involved in joint projects. Joe, Ramesh, Jack and Jill are organizationally distant from one another in varying degrees and these affiliation gaps fuel higher Virtual Distance.

Organizational distance is widespread these days because many are required to work across organizational boundaries with people who don't belong to the same organization and who are perceived to be outside "inner circles." When one belongs to one group and another to another group, people sometimes divide the world into an "us" versus "them" or "in-group" versus "out-group" mental model. It's the Yankees versus the Red Sox, only in a virtual work context.

If this kind of attitude develops, it can quickly fuel distrust and erode productivity. In the long term, organizational distance can deepen group biases. For example, those in the "in-group" think that everyone, including those in the "out-group," perceives the world the way they do when in reality, that's highly unlikely. Left unattended, organizational distance intensifies these false beliefs because it's almost impossible to accurately confirm or disconfirm any notion about others in virtual workspaces. As a result, collaboration roadblocks often lead to team failure.

For instance, in 2004, NASA launched a project to develop the Orbital Boom Sensor System, which was designed to inspect the heat-shielding tiles for damage once the shuttle was in orbit. The complex project had a strict, hard deadline—a spring 2005 launch. The NASA team in Houston subcontracted the development of a key piece of equipment, the integrated boom, to a Canadian firm. Organizational distance went unmanaged and remained high throughout the project, resulting in a loss of trust and communication. This played out when the Canadian firm fell behind schedule but never let NASA know. Because all of the pieces had to come together at the same time for the shuttle to make the launch date, the result was a project in crisis. Fortunately, the problem was resolved through the efforts of a contracting officer who served as a personal liaison or "boundary spanner" between NASA and the Canadian company. His personal relationships with people in both organizations helped to reduce some of the organizational distance that had developed, and the project was completed on schedule.

In summary, organizational distance creates an impression of space because of differences in formal associations. We find people feeling as though they're not part of the same team even though they're assigned to work together toward the same ultimate goal. Solutions to reduce organizational distance are based on the creation of a common group identity which can be shared–regardless of where team members reside or who they directly report to.

Summary—Physical Distance

Physical distance creates the sense that others are far away because, for the most part, they really are. But as we discussed, Virtual Distance can be present in just as high levels when there isn't any physical distance whatsoever. As we've discovered, the other two parts of Virtual Distance, operational and affinity distance, can play an even greater role in depressing results among the twenty-first-century virtual workforce.

OPERATIONAL DISTANCE

Operational distance (see Figure 2.3) manifests as a sense that you're on a different playing field than those you work with each and every day. For example, have you ever had

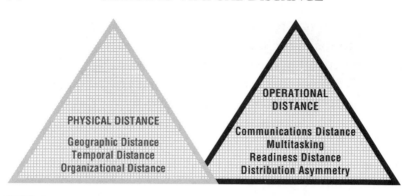

FIGURE 2.3 Operational Distance

a "conference call from hell" when, after it was over, you wondered if you lived on the same planet as the people on the other end? If so, then you were experiencing operational distance—the impression that there's no connection between you and your counterpart. Day-to-day communication problems, task overloads, technology snags like crashing hard drives and the dispersion of group members all pose major challenges and cause Virtual Distance to rise.

However, operational distance is a bit more fluid than physical distance because it's not tied to a specific place or time—it's made up of a mix of troubles that plague us from moment to moment. Operational distance, once identified, can actually be more easily controlled by team members or through management intervention.

To understand how operational distance arises, we need to take a closer look at four key issues:

1. Communications distance
2. Multitasking
3. Readiness distance
4. Distribution asymmetry

Communications Distance

Communications distance often shows up as a sense of separation from others resulting from less than meaningful interactions. For example, have you ever received an e-mail from someone and had no clue as to what they were trying to say, so you turned your attention to other things? Or perhaps you left a message for someone to answer a question, and when they responded their reply was about something completely unrelated.

When these kind of things happen to people, they often think the other person just doesn't "get it," which causes them to discount the other person or cut him out of a particular picture altogether when in fact, the reason for the miscommunication may have had nothing to do with the person's skill or abilities at all. These kinds of daily reactions, ensuing assumptions about others, and the resulting changes in behavior increase cognitive disconnects leading to increased frustration and anxiety to the individual and lower productivity for the organization.

A number of dynamics are at work in virtual workspace communications. As we've mentioned, often there aren't enough face-to-face encounters (especially across great geographic distances). When we don't share a common physical space, we don't share a common context in terms of our environment. And if we've never met, there's no way to know if we share a mental context either. And yet a shared context is the single most important part of meaningful exchange.

One of the best metaphors we've heard about the lack of a shared context among virtual team members was told to us by a former admiral from the United States Navy. At the time we spoke to him, he held a civilian post and worked on many virtual teams. But in the Navy he commanded a fleet of carriers, upon which fighter jets would land. He described his experiences with virtual team communications using the following story:

> When you're trying to communicate with someone you've never met or through channels which don't allow you to see the other person, it reminds me of trying to land a fighter jet on a naval carrier, in the middle of the ocean, at night, during a new moon. There's no darker place on earth. And as the plane approaches the ship, the pilot can't see a thing. He or she has no sense of where they are in relation to the deck. They lose all depth perception. When I'm on a videoconference or trying to glean what someone means from an e-mail, it's like trying to land a fighter plane onto the carrier deck on a black sea in the middle of the night. I have no depth perception. And worse, I'm flying without any instruments at all.

When we try to communicate virtually and don't share a common context, we're basically flying blind with respect to what others are trying to convey. Without a sense of where the person is (uneven environmental factors such as varied temperatures, lighting, sound, or physical comfort, etc.) or what they might be thinking (differences in worldviews, variations in preexisting assumptions, their current "mood," etc.), it's almost impossible to interpret his intended meaning.

But even when we're physically close, communications distance can grow. One of our favorite stories about "same place" communication distance was told to us by a woman who worked in an insurance company where the cubicles were no more than 12 inches apart. Her boss sat right next to her and, unbelievably, would actually e-mail her questions instead of just turning around and talking to her directly. He did this constantly, creating a psychological gulf between them that felt to her like "a huge valley between mountain ranges."

In summary, communications distance turns into a feeling of disconnectedness when there's a lack of shared context and when a less than optimal communication mode is used repeatedly. Therefore, the way to close communications distance involves developing common ideas about the places and ways in which we work as well as more selectively using various kinds of communications tools and techniques.

Multitasking

Multitasking increases Virtual Distance because when occupied with many and varied tasks, we tend to feel far away from pretty much everything. We're so focused on the activity that others often get pushed aside in our minds. And there isn't a person we know who isn't overwhelmed with things to do these days. Because we *can* do more, we're doing more. But there are limits. In his 1990 book, *Flow: The Psychology of Optimal Experience*, Mihaly Csikszentmihalyi described these boundaries:

> The limitation of consciousness is demonstrated by the fact that to understand what another person is saying we must process 40 bits of information each second. If we assume the upper limit of our capacity to be 126 bits per second, it follows that to understand what three people are saying simultaneously is theoretically possible, but only by managing to keep out of consciousness every other thought or sensation. We couldn't, for instance, be aware of the speakers' expressions, nor could we wonder about why they are saying what they are saying, or notice what they are wearing.

Of course Csikszentmihalyi himself wrote that these were just approximations. But what he described as the limits of consciousness in 1990 is being further studied by neuroscientists today.

Dr. Martin Westwell[3] discovered that interruptions from too much electronic communications disturb us most when we're engaged in difficult or "cognitively demanding" tasks like problem solving.[4] And yet, it is problem solving, which requires intense thought, that's at the center of building competitive advantage. So when people get to the point that they're tasked to the max, especially at inopportune times, companies may be thwarting their own innovations and future success.

According to Westwell, multitasking and information overload impede the brain's executive function, the part which decides what's meaningful and what's not; what to pay attention to and what to ignore. When overloaded, we can develop autistic-like behaviors because our own internal executive function is unable to discern background noise from things that are truly important. When this happens, our decision-making and innovative skills suffer.

In summary, too much multitasking creates a sense of distance between us. However, as you'll see in Chapter 3, this matters *most* when Virtual Distance is high in other areas. Solutions to reduce over-activity rest with the individual. People need to make better decisions about what to work on, when, and set boundaries for themselves on how much time they'll spend on any given endeavor. Managers also have a role to play by actively taking notice of when team members are overburdened and remove things from their plates or else Virtual Distance will increase.

Readiness Distance

Readiness distance is the feeling of detachment that grows when technical support can't fix problems with machines and other devices in a timely manner. Most likely, you've already experienced readiness distance. It would've happened while you waited for a technical glitch to be fixed during a videoconference, a webinar, a conference call, a presentation, a demonstration of software, or some other technically dependent event.

Readiness distance produces a "mind drift" in team members when technical issues preclude them from getting work done. If the problem lasts more than a minute or so, they begin to psychologically separate from those who are also waiting, and if it persists, projects can be temporarily derailed. In some cases it can lead to lasting and more permanent problems.

For example, at a large pharmaceutical firm headquartered in the northeastern United States, readiness distance created high levels of Virtual Distance. It began when an initiative was launched to reorganize global operations into a single hierarchal unit. During the transition, the head of Australian operations needed a conference call facility to conduct meetings with his teams in Australia and the Far East. To put such a communication line in place under the new structure, he had to work with the technical staff in the United States.

But when he asked them to carry out his request, the U.S. technical manager informed him that, "We are closed during the hours you want to have your meetings, so we can't support you. You'll have to change the time of your meeting to get conference lines."

In disbelief, the Australian executive e-mailed back, "But those are our daytime work hours. We've got to be able to get conference calls during those hours!" The technical manager replied, "Well, we're not a 24/7 shop and I've got no budget to pay someone to be here for you at that time. Without support, we can't set up a line."

This readiness distance interjected Virtual Distance between the Australian leader and the U.S. headquarters at precisely the wrong time—when high levels of cooperation were needed most. Only intervention by the most senior executives in the United States eventually fixed the situation, but the damage was done. The relationship between the Australian executive and some U.S. counterparts was never fully repaired, and a lasting Virtual Distance ensued.

In summary, readiness distance rises when things don't work and there's little to no support or cooperation. The solutions to readiness distance revolve around ensuring that the right foundational structures are in place and that individuals are ready when they're needed most.

Distribution Asymmetry

Distribution asymmetry is an uneven dispersion of people within any given team or organization. This patchy array of resources causes people to feel as though they're further away than they may really be. In one case, teams consist of a lot of individuals working remotely in their homes or other non-corporate locations. This situation often produces a sense of isolation among individuals. In another case, distribution asymmetry can arise when there are a lot of people located in one centralized place, like a headquarter location. And in a third case, both high dispersion and high centralization can exist within the same team; some members in the hinterlands and some at headquarters. In this case, not only can far-flung resources feel isolated, but those at headquarters usually become somewhat cocooned and have trouble seeing beyond their own views.

Companies like the pharmaceutical organization described in the last example had a large population of headquartered personnel. When they began their globalization effort, many outside of that environment felt that their views were not considered. And among the people in the headquarter location, some admitted they defended points of view that probably didn't reflect the group as a whole.

In summary, distribution asymmetry creates a sense of being far away from others either by virtue of isolation or too many people residing in one place where there's a lot of power. Resolutions to distribution asymmetry are not always easy to find. However, the effects of distribution asymmetry are often mitigated by reducing Virtual Distance in other areas.

Summary—Operational Distance

Operational distance causes people to mentally shut others out as they try to make their way through harried and sometimes difficult days. Most of the time, operational distance intensifies without conscious awareness. However, we know that it does a lot of harm. But, out of all the pieces in the Virtual Distance Model, operational distance is the most easily controlled by an alert and skilled management.

AFFINITY DISTANCE

Affinity distance (see Figure 2.4) is what develops when we don't establish the kinds of personal relationships that satisfy

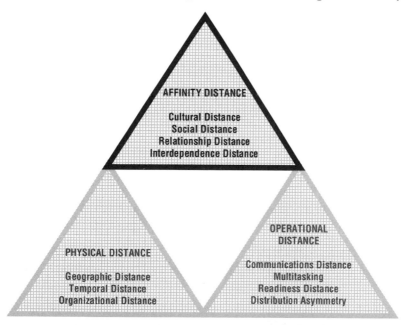

FIGURE 2.4 Affinity Distance

our social needs. When this facet of Virtual Distance is high, a powerful psychological wall bars effective collaboration.

In business relationships, it's affinity that holds teams together despite location, nationality, or organizational affiliation. The absence of affinity, or a weak affinity, has the strongest influence on Virtual Distance. When people can't attach themselves to one another, then work suffers. There's no reason, for example, to commit wholeheartedly to any given initiative. Managers and individuals alike often tell us they have trouble motivating those whom they don't see or aren't directly in their span of influence or control.

And most of the time it's because there's no affinity in the group. Therefore, reducing affinity distance is the most important undertaking for team members and management. When successful, the other two Virtual Distance issues, physical and operational distance, are also reduced.

There are four relationship dynamics that come together to create an affinity vacuum:

1. Cultural distance
2. Social distance
3. Relationship distance
4. Interdependence distance

Cultural Distance

Cultural distance represents differences in team member values (the internal rules or guidelines that direct our lives and decision making), which come in many forms and are described in Figure 2.5.

Affinity is difficult if not impossible to establish if some or all of our values are out of sync.

For instance, we were involved in a project for the Port Authority of New York and New Jersey. The objective was to find out how communications in New York

Moral values—personal set of absolute values used as a guide to know what is "right" versus "wrong." When these are violated, we tend to take drastic action. Whistleblowers exemplify when moral values have been crossed at work.

Work values—the internal road map we create to guide us through work made up of our personal values as they are applied to our individual work habits and styles.

Personal values—the internal road map we create for ourselves based on internalization of group values combined with our own unique worldviews

Cultural Values—group values that arise from being part of various communities both at home and at work

FIGURE 2.5 Values Stack

City could be improved between a combination of federal, state, and city agencies to avoid future disasters. Interestingly, we found that cultural distance stemming from different organizational values (e.g., secrecy versus openness) between agencies charged with coordinating future security was entrenched in bureaucratic structures. In fact, this was the most serious obstacle to developing open and effective relations.[5]

Varied work values among team members also cause problems through something as simple as differences in communication styles. For instance, a client in Europe had difficulties over e-mail with North American counterparts because of the meaning attributed not to the words but to the writing style itself. The Europeans wrote short, to-the-point messages that the North Americans misinterpreted as harsh and even rude because they wrote in a more friendly and conversational style.

In summary, cultural distance is at the top of the list when it comes to escalating affinity distance and stunting healthy relationship growth in the virtual workforce. Fixing cultural distance consists of developing shared value systems and re-imagining values in light of others that may appear to be different but, in many ways, are much the same.

Social Distance

Social distance develops when people hold a range of different social positions. Status within and across groups is relevant to any form of collaboration. For example, people have different levels of status in local communities, and these striations are influenced by factors such as political position and wealth, among others. The truth is that some get more consideration than others, fostering a sense of unfairness that increases social distance.

Similarly, status differences exist within organizations; those with higher formal status tend to be more politically powerful and influential. The further away on a "status scale" people are from one another, the further away they may perceive themselves to be in any given collaborative effort. This generates social distance within an organizational context.

Deemphasizing formal status and fanning contributions of team members by building up their social capital within the team is vital. In the virtual workforce, companies are usually trying to get people to think of each other as peers and behave in a cooperative manner. But most companies still use titles and hierarchies in order to delineate who is most important. When formal status is emphasized, as opposed to the contributions each team member makes to the group effort, major productivity issues can arise.

A case in point appeared at a major bank based in New York. Many of their information technology (IT) divisions use resources from different countries where formal status is very important. One way in which respect is shown to superior classes is by agreeing with everything they say, no matter what the person in the lower class really thinks. The answer to every question asked by a higher class person is "yes."

This practice found its way into the bank, and given this behavior, those lower in title and position rarely speak up about work problems. Since they hardly ever bring anything to management's attention, it often happens that projects fall behind schedule and over budget. In one case, social distance problems caused a multimillion-dollar project to be scrapped and wiped out all the savings the organization hoped to realize.

In summary, it's easy to see how harmful social distance can be and how difficult it is to manage, as it involves identity and ego, two of the most fragile aspects of human psychology. However, when team members feel they're on a level playing field based on competence and their shared role in the work effort, they're much more likely to meet goals. So to decrease social distance, managers need to encourage open communications and create meritocracies where individuals and peers share a sense of being valued by the group

Relationship Distance

Relationship distance is the extent to which you and others lack relationship connections from past work initiatives. If you belong to any kind of online social networking system, you can usually see pictures that show the number of direct ties you have with someone and the number of indirect ties with many others. These relationships, known as strong ties and weak ties, respectively, are needed for healthy communications and relationship building. When there are no historical ties between two or more people or only a scattered few, than one feels more distant from the rest.

When 9/11 occurred in New York, the central communication switches servicing the World Trade Center area had been either destroyed or severely interrupted. Miles away, an emergency response team was gathered in New Jersey. Led by one of the financial officers of the telecommunications provider, a group of senior managers, who'd worked together previously, was quickly assembled on the front lawn of the company's main campus. Tables were set up, with different teams manning different operational centers. Leaders selected individuals for those teams based mostly on whether they'd worked together in the past—especially during other kinds of crises. In other cases, people who were chosen for critical assignments were referred by trusted colleagues. The company succeeded in getting service back up and running relatively quickly given the gravity of the situation. Low relationship distance was one of the main reasons why people could come together quickly, communicate effectively, and solve problems rapidly.

In summary, relationship distance manifests as a sense of unfamiliarity. When people don't have any idea of who others are or lack any indirect connections, it's difficult to establish trust without having to build a relationship from scratch, and as we've learned already, our ability to do so in the Digital Age is challenged quite a bit by forces outside of our control, for example, being near or having time to devote to such efforts. The solutions to relationship distance are tied to creating an alert management that can seed teams or groups with people who already know each other or know some of the same people. As we'll see in Chapter 5, there are also other ways to help people develop social networks.

Interdependence Distance

Interdependence distance describes the psychology behind team member commitment to one another—or a lack thereof. If individuals or groups don't believe they're mutually dependent on each other, then motivation wanes and projects drift. When there is no shared vision or linked missions, a feeling of "not being part of the action," so to speak, sabotages the desire to actively participate.

One of the major problems in outsourcing relationships is interdependence distance. In 2005, a large credit card company had a major security breach when an outsourcing provider sent portions of the work to another outsourcer. While the card company had negotiated a contract that included a governance structure to keep interdependence high between the two parties, there was little in the contract that tied the card company to other outsourcing companies "downstream." The breach in security was a result of one of these relationships gone awry, where there was no interdependence whatsoever between the customer and the smaller outsourcer hired by the main service provider. As a result, the chief technology architect of the credit card company told a group of financial services executives that the problem was becoming so prevalent that they gave it a name, "Interdependence Risk," which is now formally used as an indicator of potential financial and reputation exposure in many major financial institutions.

In summary, interdependence distance can hurt companies quite badly because people are too detached from one another—not in terms of physicality but in terms of their connection to a shared vision. Managers need to create a sense of interdependence between team members because it's often too difficult or unclear from the individual's point of view.

Summary—Affinity Distance

Affinity distance arises from a lack of commonality between our values systems and styles, social behaviors, relationship histories, and worldviews or mental pictures of the world. The four affinity distance areas represent those dynamics that shape us as human beings. They provide the context in which we develop and retain relationships; therefore, within virtual teamwork, it's of primary importance to reduce affinity distance.

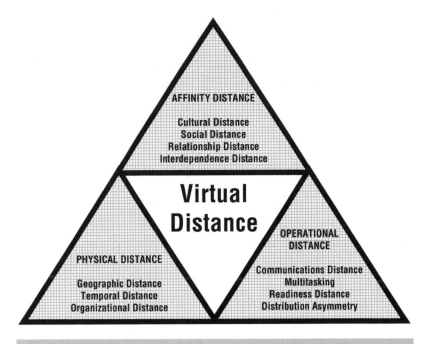

FIGURE 2.6 The Virtual Distance Model

THE VIRTUAL DISTANCE MODEL: PUTTING IT ALL TOGETHER

We've now met Virtual Distance (see Figure 2.6). It's a model made up of a trio of distance-causing features in the virtual workplace, each of which can be active one at a time, but more often than not, all at the same time. Let's go back to our CIO who had spent three years using over 50 success criteria to understand his global portfolio of projects. In most of them, multiple locations, miscommunications, and a cadre of people who didn't know each other, among other things, were part and parcel to the problems. By sorting these many varied quandaries into their respective corners of the Virtual Distance Model, he had a much clearer view of why projects stood where they did.

But the challenge of fixing problems among the virtual workforce doesn't stop there. It is incumbent upon anyone trying to reduce Virtual Distance to go further and measure the extent to which it is impacting important outcomes. That's where the Virtual Distance Index and other Virtual Distance metrics come in.

NOTES

1. Charles H. House, *Building Effective Virtual Teams*, (presentation on August 1, 2007, at Stanford University, Media X Summer Institute).

2. Mitzi M. Montoya-Weiss, Anne P. Massey, and Michael Song, Getting it together: Temporal coordination and conflict management in global virtual teams, *Academy of Management Journal* 44 (2001): 1251-62.

3. Former Director for the Future of the Mind at Oxford University and now the Director of Flinders Centre for Science Education in the 21st Century at Flinders University in Adelaide, Australia.

4. M. Westwell, Disruptive communication and attentive productivity, *Institute for the Future of the Mind* (University of Oxford, 2007).

5. Stevens Institute of Technology, *Securing the Port of New York and New Jersey: Network-Centric Operations Applied to the Campaign Against Terrorism, September 2004*, www.stevens.edu.

～ 3 ～

Measuring Virtual Distance

There are some startling statistical results that have been uncovered between Virtual Distance and several important organizational outcomes. In the first study we conducted, a variety of data was collected from over 300 different projects, and Virtual Distance was measured within each of these. A variety of different kinds of projects in a wide mix of industries were included. Our objective was to see if we could empirically verify the relationship between Virtual Distance and organizational performance. We used a technique called linear modeling to link the Virtual Distance pieces to critical success factors. We designed our formula to incorporate all three distance facets of the Virtual Distance Model: physical, operational, and affinity. The model provides an overall Virtual Distance Index (VDI), where higher scores mean greater Virtual Distance. The formula took the following form:

$$P_{success} = W_3 Physical + W_2 Operational + W_1 Affinity$$

Here, the W's represent the weights for each type of distance. We found that as Virtual Distance got lower, project results were better, as represented in Figure 3.1.

One of the companies we studied was an organization that made a conscious decision to collocate all of its

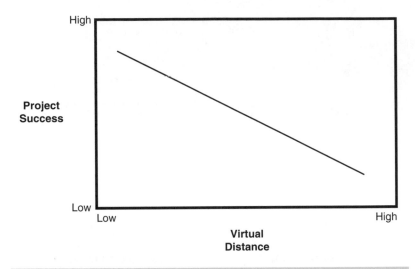

FIGURE 3.1 Virtual Distance and Project Success

employees. While, as expected, there was little Virtual Distance from physical factors, we were surprised to discover that operational and affinity distance factors in this case created almost as much Virtual Distance as we found in globally distributed teams. What's more, we saw that success of projects in this organization was highly correlated with the degree of Virtual Distance operating within the project teams.

Simply showing that Virtual Distance is predictive of success doesn't tell much of a story, however. It's a black box. We know it works, but we don't know why.

Fortunately, we were able to measure a number of other key indicators that helped us understand how Virtual Distance works. The important indicators that we looked at included:

- *Trust.* The degree that people trusted one another
- *Innovative behavior.* The extent to which people were working in innovative ways
- *Organizational citizenship.* The degree to which people engaged in voluntary behaviors like helping and sharing information

- *Satisfaction.* The extent to which people were satisfied with their participation in the project
- *Vision clarity.* The extent to which people understood and shared a common vision for the project

VIRTUAL DISTANCE AND TRUST

When we interact with other people in a work setting we process interactions in two ways: analytically and emotionally. So it's not surprising that studies have identified two types of trust: cognitive trust and affective trust. As Virtual Distance increases, our trust becomes more cognitively based. There are no personal ties and no relationship, so we trust based on the rational belief that others will behave in a trustworthy manner. As Virtual Distance is lowered, our trust becomes more affectively based. It also should be no surprise that cognitively based trust tends to be more fragile than affectively based trust. In other words, it's easier to go from a trusting to a distrusting relationship when the basis is purely rational. We could say the same for relationships that are primarily virtual. Another interviewee offered some insight into why this might be the case:

> The problem with working with people at distant locations is one of communication on a lower level. One may establish better working relationships with people on the same location through personal contact. Without this relationship, people at distant locations are less likely to consider requests for information to be important, and misunderstandings may result.

Depending on their personality, people vary in the extent to which they are trusting of coworkers, managers, and organizations.[1] This personality factor is called *propensity to trust* and has been shown to be a good predictor of trust in organizational settings.[2] All other things being equal, if you're going to hire people to work together, it's better to have people who are high in propensity to trust. The odds are good that they'll all end up trusting one another. This is especially true in virtual settings. In another of the studies that we conducted,[3] we looked at the extent to which pairs of coworkers trusted one another. Propensity to trust was much more important when the two coworkers were working virtually than when they were collocated.

However, there are three other important factors that lead to the development of trusting relationships. They are benevolence, ability, and integrity. The more I think that my coworkers have my best interests at heart (benevolence), the more likely I am to trust them. The more I think that my coworkers have the knowledge and ability to get the job done (ability), the more likely I am to trust them. The more I think that my coworkers will do what they promise (integrity), the more likely I am to trust them. All three of these influencers are based on information that we have about our coworkers. This information can come from prior relationships or what other people tell us, or, more likely, it comes from our own experience.

As we found, Virtual Distance influences not only how much people trust one another, but also how much they see their coworkers as being benevolent, as having integrity, and as having the requisite ability. Figure 3.2 shows that all three of the critical factors are strongly influenced by Virtual Distance.

TRUST AND THE SECRET OF LIFE

In the early 1950s, two British scientists were working on a problem fundamental to our understanding of human life. According to most accounts, James Watson and Francis Crick, who won the Nobel Prize for medicine for their discovery of the structure of DNA, owed their success to work done by Maurice Wilkins and Rosalind Franklin, physical chemists who worked in a nearby laboratory. Franklin was known to both Crick and Watson, but not very well. The bridge was Maurice Wilkins, who had strong ties with Crick and Watson and knew Franklin quite well. Wilkins trusted Watson and Crick enough to share a photograph that Franklin took using X-ray crystallography, which showed that DNA was a double helix and confirmed for the first time the hypothesis that Crick and Watson had proposed. This led to Crick's announcement that they had found "the secret of life."

Trust is a bit like the glue that holds teams and organizations together. Without it, teams become less productive, people are less willing to share information and help one another, and energy that could be spent on innovation is spent on avoiding perceived threats from others. We will discuss some of the influences of trust in more detail in the rest of this chapter, but it was clear from our research that the same factors that produce Virtual Distance also lower trust. When Virtual Distance is high, trust is in short supply (see Figure 3.3), so it is no wonder that many organizations

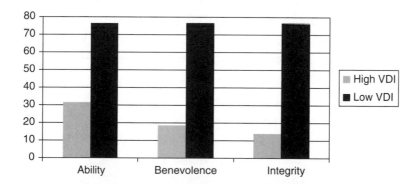

FIGURE 3.2 Virtual Distance and Ability, Benevolence, and Integrity When Virtual Distance is low (Low VDI), team members are rated high on ability, benevolence, and integrity. But when Virtual Distance is high (High VDI), team members are rated significantly lower on the same three factors.

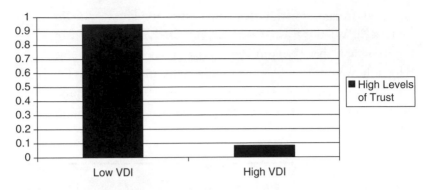

FIGURE 3.3 Virtual Distance and Trust
Among those who scored low on Virtual Distance (Low VDI), over 90% felt there was a high level of trust among team members. Among those who scored high on Virtual Distance (High VDI), less than 10% felt there was a high level of trust among team members.

are trying to find solutions to managing globally distributed teams.

VIRTUAL DISTANCE AND INNOVATION

At this point, you may still be skeptical as to why we think trust is so important. Let's start with one of the most important aspects of work today—innovation. In 2003, PricewaterhouseCoopers conducted a survey on innovation across many different companies. Here's a direct quote from the PWC report: "At the heart of the issues impacting how people work together is trust. Of the quantitative data in the survey, trust between people which enabled them to share ideas freely was the *single most significant factor* in differentiating successful innovators."[4]

How is trust related to innovation? There are at least three connections: cross-fertilization, constructive criticism, and acceptance of failure. First, a lot of good ideas, if not most, come from the cross–fertilization that we get when we talk with customers, colleagues, coworkers, or people in other disciplines. This cross-fertilization occurs only when people are comfortable sharing information. But sharing information makes us vulnerable. We might be ridiculed, or someone might steal our idea or take credit for it. In their discovery of the double helix, Wilkins trusted Crick and Watson and shared some information with them that led to the discovery of the structure of DNA. Crick and Watson ended up citing Wilkins and Franklin in their published work. What did Wilkins get for trusting Crick and Watson? He shared with them in the 1962 Nobel Prize for medicine!

A second connection is that ideas get better when they're debated, built on, and discussed within a constructive framework. The two types of conflict that we see when people work together—task-related (good) and personal (bad)—have been compared for teams that have different levels of trust. Without trust, conversations that involve task-related conflict and argument may not occur or, if they do occur, can quickly turn into personal conflict. The research shows that when trust is high within a team, task-related conflict is much less likely to deteriorate into conflict that is personal in nature.[5]

Finally, innovation involves taking risks and occasionally failing. Employees have to trust that failure is okay or they won't take any risks. However, management has to trust employees enough to give them the freedom to come up with new ideas. One of the most innovative companies in the world, the 3M Corporation, trusts its employees enough to allow them to use up to 15 percent of their time to work on their own innovative ideas.[6]

Figure 3.3 illustrates how dramatically Virtual Distance influences the level of trust. High Virtual Distance = low trust. This makes sense not only because of the empirical data, but also from a logical viewpoint. Physical distance

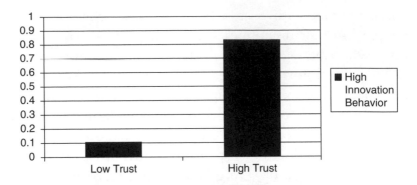

FIGURE 3.4 Trust and Innovation
Among those who rated trust low (Low Trust), less than 10% say they exhibit innovative behaviors. Among those who rated trust high (High Trust), over 80% say they exhibit high innovative behaviors.

lowers the degree of social presence that is critical for building relationships and trust. As we discuss later, social presence is the sense that you're connected to and with the other person. Operational distance—communicating through technology rather than face to face—for example, limits the extent to which relationships can be formed and strengthened over time. Finally, affinity distance goes to the heart of trusting relationships. When we have different values and communication styles and lack common relationships, it's difficult to build trust. Figure 3.4 shows how trust and innovation are related.

Higher trust leads to more innovative behavior. But this is only part of the story. Virtual Distance not only drives trust, which drives innovation, but Virtual Distance has an additional effect on innovation over and above the influence on trust. We tested the model shown in Figure 3.5 and found that Virtual Distance influences innovation in two ways. First, it influences trust, which in turn influences innovation. This is called an indirect effect. But Virtual Distance also has an additional direct effect on innovation.

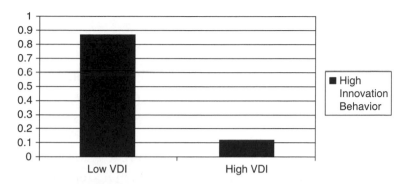

FIGURE 3.5 Virtual Distance and Innovation
Among those who rated Virtual Distance low (Low VDI), over 80%
felt that innovative behavior was high among team members. Among
those who rated Virtual Distance high (High VDI), only slightly more
than 10% felt that innovative behaviors were high among team
members.

If we consider both the direct and indirect influence that
Virtual Distance has on innovation, it's clear that lowering
Virtual Distance is important if you want innovation to happen. As employees become more distributed, organizations
are struggling with the innovation challenge. One company
that had a highly distributed new product development organization went so far as to relocate all of its employees into
a common, specially designed building at a cost of over $7
million in an effort to boost innovation. Of course, collocation removes the physical dimension of Virtual Distance
but not necessarily the operational and affinity factors.

VIRTUAL DISTANCE AND
ORGANIZATIONAL CITIZENSHIP

A woman at State Farm Mutual Insurance Co. was converting a
paper database into an electronic one. "Why are you working so
energetically?" someone asked her. "Don't you know that you
are working yourself out of a job?" "Sure," she answered, "but
I've been here long enough to know that I can trust them. They'll

find something else for me. If I didn't believe that, I might be
tempted to sabotage the process."[7]

Organizational citizenship behavior (OCB) includes all
those behaviors that are not strictly required by a job description. Some of these behaviors have an altruistic nature.
Examples include helping others with their work, sharing
information, giving time to help teammates, and encouraging teammates when they're down. Others reflect "civic
virtue" and include keeping up with developments in the
organization and attending functions and meetings that are
not required. OCB has a negative side as well. We all know
employees who are constantly complaining about trivial
matters, making problems bigger than they really are, and
always focusing on the negative side of things. The negative behaviors can escalate to destructive behaviors, such
as sabotage or even outright theft. One study showed that
thefts increased when organizations communicated a pay
reduction in a way that engendered distrust.[8]

As our State Farm employee illustrates, the level of trust
can set the context for either positive or negative OCB.
Figure 3.6 shows how trust is related to OCB.

High levels of trust allow people to focus on the work
that needs to be done without worrying about someone else
undermining their work or falsely taking credit for something. When we trust our coworkers, we don't think twice
about sharing information or going out of our way to help
someone else. These kinds of behaviors only increase in
importance as we move increasingly toward networked and
team-based structures.

Virtual Distance can influence OCB in two ways. Because it influences trust and trust influences OCB, it has
an indirect effect. But it also has a direct effect. Figure 3.7
shows the difference between participants in our research
who had high or low Virtual Distance and the level of OCB
behavior that they reported.

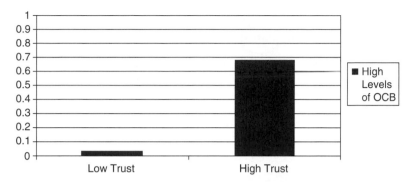

FIGURE 3.6 Trust and Organizational Citizenship Behaviors
Among those who rated trust among team members low (Low Trust),
less than 5% said that they felt team members exhibited high levels of
organizational citizenship and helping behaviors. Among those who
rated trust among team members high (High Trust), almost 70% felt
team members exhibited high levels of organizational citizenship and
helping behaviors.

High levels of OCB not only make working more pleas-
ant and rewarding, but also lead to better performance. In
a study of factory production teams, OCB led to both better quality and higher productivity.[9] Another study showed

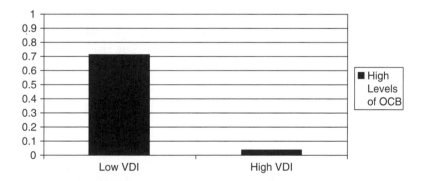

FIGURE 3.7 Virtual Distance and Organizational Citizenship
Among those who scored low on Virtual Distance (Low VDI), over
70% felt that team members exhibited high organizational citizenship
and helping behaviors. Among those who scored high on Virtual
Distance (High VDI), less than 5% felt that team members exhibited
high organizational citizenship and helping behaviors.

similar results for the performance of projects.[10] Finally, we'll present results later in this chapter from our own data that show a strong relationship between OCB and project success.

VIRTUAL DISTANCE AND SATISFACTION

Usually, when people are asked why they work, one answer seems obvious—for the money. While it is true that pay (and benefits) are important, the research tells us that we can be satisfied or dissatisfied for several other reasons. Three of the most important reasons are the quality of our leadership, how much we enjoy the actual work, and interactions with our coworkers. Having a great manager can make us look forward to coming to work each day, and having a miserable manager can make work intolerable. Likewise, having work that fully engages us can make the day go faster and give us a sense of accomplishment. And having great coworkers can be a source of real enjoyment and meet our need for social interaction.

We were interested in how working virtually affected satisfaction, particularly when we looked at the comments from the people we interviewed. We got a variety of opinions, such as the following: "The same location promotes interaction and teamwork, especially for a dedicated cross-functional project"; and "Working in the same location is better. It allows for face-to-face meetings between individuals and/or teams as may be needed to solve problems and answer questions. Communication between team members is faster when working in the same environment."

However, we also got this comment: "Distance is not a problem. I am on the best team; have the kindest, most considerate coworkers imaginable; and a great leader who is always positive and supportive. We are all very lucky."

So we were curious to see whether it was collocation or Virtual Distance that made the difference in job satisfaction. We asked our participants to rate their agreement on the following four questions:

1. I would enjoy working with the same team members again.
2. I enjoyed working with the project manager on this project.
3. The work on this project was enjoyable.
4. I was satisfied with the reward or compensation that I received for working on this project.

We quickly found that collocation, by itself, had nothing to do with any of the aspects of satisfaction we asked about. We then examined the relationship between Virtual Distance and each of the four aspects of satisfaction. We did not find any relationship with pay, but then we were not expecting one, since pay should not be affected by Virtual Distance. For the other three items, however, the relationships were all significant. Figure 3.8 shows how Virtual Distance is related to each of the satisfaction indices.

Clearly, as Virtual Distance becomes lower, people are more satisfied with their coworkers, their boss, and the nature of the work that they're doing.

Why should we care about satisfaction? There are several reasons. First, since almost all of work is done virtually to some extent and we spend a good deal of our waking hours engaged in work, it's important to know that the same factors that lower Virtual Distance will tend to make us more satisfied. The factors that are related to affinity distance are particularly important. Working with people with whom we share the same values and communication style and having a sense of interdependence will lower Virtual Distance and make our working experiences more enjoyable.

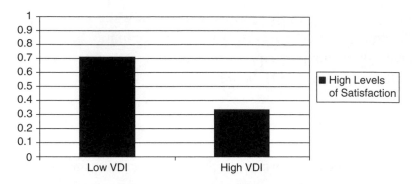

FIGURE 3.8 Virtual Distance and Satisfaction
Among those who scored low on Virtual Distance (Low VDI), over 70% were highly satisfied with their work and other team members. Among those who scored high on Virtual Distance (High VDI), only about 30% were highly satisfied with their work and other team members.

From an organizational perspective, we know that satisfied employees are more likely to stay with the company, thus reducing recruiting and selection costs. Satisfied employees also create what are called "spillover effects," such as helping to recruit job candidates, recommending company products and services, and generally creating goodwill toward the company. Finally, satisfaction does have a slight but significant relationship with productivity. In general, more satisfied employees tend to be more productive. By increasing satisfaction, lowering Virtual Distance can actually improve the bottom line.

VIRTUAL DISTANCE AND CLARITY OF VISION

In Chapter 2, we discussed how Virtual Distance created a problem in a NASA project. Some background may be helpful in understanding how a clear vision made this project ultimately successful. On February 1, 2003, the orbiter module for the Space Shuttle *Columbia* was destroyed because of damage to its thermal control system. All seven crew members were killed. Within hours of this disaster, the *Columbia* Accident Investigation Board (CAIB) was formed, and in August 2003, they issued their report. Among the recommendations made by the CAIB was the development of a system for inspecting the tiles in the thermal shield once the orbiter module began orbiting the earth. On September 3, 2003, the Orbiter Boom Sensor System (OBSS) project began at the Johnson Space Center. The OBSS project not only met an extremely aggressive schedule, but produced an innovative solution to a significant problem in the space shuttle program. One of the major reasons for that success was the clarity of vision established at the very outset.

The vision for the product was clear from the first stages of the project. "Develop a capability for inspecting damage to the Orbiter TPS while in orbit." The vision was clear and accepted as a given by all project team members interviewed, although there were still some uncertainties at the time of our interviews with the project team. Two of the most critical concerns were (1) the technical requirements for the laser sensors; and (2) the ability to repair tile damage if it is detected. Members of the project team understood and accepted these uncertainties and did not let them interfere with their objectives. All team members expressed a high level of commitment to the project and underscored its importance to resuming shuttle operations. For example, "the OBSS will have a capability of detecting damage to a depth of 0.25 inch." The vision for the team was clear, and within the specified design parameters, team members were empowered to make decisions, problem solve, and be innovative. This empowerment contributed to the sense of ownership and high level of commitment on the part of team members.

The OBSS is an example of how clarity of vision can provide the basis for success. Clarity of vision means that everyone on the project team understands the goals of the project, what needs to be done, how it should be done, and who needs to do it. The problem we described in Chapter 2 was solved by reducing Virtual Distance and getting the Canadian subcontractor on the same page as the rest of the team. Team researchers use a closely allied concept "shared mental model" to describe a quality that most high-performing teams have. They know how the team interacts, who has specific knowledge and expertise, and how information can be shared and communicated.

The NASA project is not the only one in which clarity of vision was important. In our research on over 700 new product development teams, we found clarity of vision to be the single most important differentiator between successful and unsuccessful projects.[11] We had not yet looked at one important question. How did distance affect clarity of vision?

We first looked at collocation alone to see if it had any influence on the clarity of vision. It didn't. But Virtual Distance had a dramatic effect on vision clarity. Figure 3.9

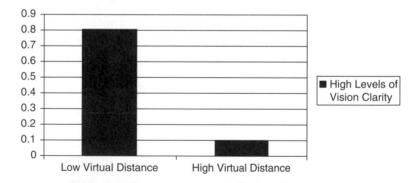

FIGURE 3.9 Virtual Distance and Vision Clarity
Among those who scored low on Virtual Distance (Low Virtual Distance), 80% felt that there was clarity among team members about the vision of the project or work initiative. Among those who scored high on Virtual Distance (High Virtual Distance), only 10% felt that there was clarity among team members about the vision of the project or work initiative.

shows the difference in vision clarity for the lowest 25 percent in Virtual Distance and the highest 25 percent in Virtual Distance.

In the low Virtual Distance group, 80% were high in vision clarity as compared with slightly less than 10% in the high Virtual Distance group. The same factors that lower Virtual Distance, especially affinity distance and operational distance, also serve to increase the clarity of vision and produce a shared mental model.

PUTTING IT ALL TOGETHER: VIRTUAL DISTANCE AND SUCCESS

We have shown how Virtual Distance influences trust, innovation, organizational citizenship, satisfaction, and clarity of vision. Based on our analysis and our experience with a number of organizations, the implications of Virtual Distance for companies are obvious and will only continue to grow in importance as we become more distributed, networked, and project based. Figure 3.10 shows how

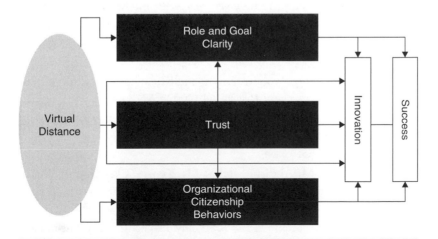

FIGURE 3.10 How Virtual Distance Impacts Success

Virtual Distance influences project success through the other variables that we studied.

Virtual Distance has important consequences for today's organizations. Trust, innovation, organizational citizenship, job satisfaction, and vision clarity are keys to performance and success. Lowering Virtual Distance has a positive impact on all of these. However, the measures alone don't help us to pinpoint exactly where Virtual Distance lives among team members, who it's impacting most, and what areas to concentrate on fixing first. That's where Virtual Distance Mapping comes in and is the subject of the next chapter.

NOTES

1. P. Dasgupta. Trust as a commodity, in *Trust,* ed. D. G. Gambetta (New York: Basil Blackwell, 1988) 49–72.

2. R. Mayer, J. Davis, and D. Schoorman, An integrative model of organizational trust, *Academy of Management Review,* 20 (1995): 709–34.

3. M. Yakovleva, R. Reilly, and R. Werko, Understanding trust: A dyadic analysis (Presented at Society of Industrial and Organizational Psychology, San Francisco, CA, April, 2007).

4. Price Waterhouse Coopers, *Innovation Survey*, (London: 2003).

5. R. R. Reilly, (ed.). *The Human Side of Project Leadership.* (Kennett Square, PA: Project Management Institute. 2007)

6. Adam Brand, Knowledge management and innovation at 3M. *Journal of Knowledge Management,* 2 (1998): 17–22.

7. Henry Mintzberg, Robert Simon, and Kunal Basu, Beyond selfishness, *Sloan Management Review,* 44 (2002): 67–74.

8. J. Greenberg, Employee theft as a reaction to underpayment inequity: The hidden cost of pay cuts, *Journal of Applied Psychology*, 75 (1990) 561–568.

9. P. Podsakoff, M. Ahearne, and S. MacKenzie, Organizational citizenship behavior and the quantity and quality of work group performance, *Journal of Applied Psychology*, 82 (1997) 262–70.

10. Z. Aronson, A. Shenhar, and R. Reilly, Project spirit and its impact on project success, *The Human Side of Project Leadership.* (Kennett Square, PA: Project Management Institute, 2007).

11. For example, in new product development we found that Clarity of Vision during the new product development stage was the most important factor in separating the award winning new products from the moderately successful and unsuccessful products. See Gary Lynn and Richard Reilly, *Blockbusters: Developing Award Winning New Products* (New York: Harper-Collins, 2002).

~ 4 ~

Mapping Virtual Distance

Virtual Distance, as we saw in Chapter 3, can have a significant impact on organizational performance and individual job satisfaction. But it's difficult to know where to start in terms of addressing Virtual Distance problems more directly without more information. For example, we can take a survey and know that in the aggregate, Virtual Distance contributes to lost revenues, lower innovation, or reputation damage. But to fix it and manage it into the future, we need to know more about the exact location of Virtual Distance problems.

It's kind of like thinking about air traffic. We know that at any given point in time there are lots of planes in the air. But to avoid problems like near misses, air traffic controllers need to know exactly where each plane is, how high it's flying, what other planes are in the nearby vicinity, and so forth. With this information, they can safely guide planes into and out of the airport and keep track of them as they make their way to their final destinations.

Managers are like the air traffic controllers in terms of Virtual Distance. While it's important for them to know whether Virtual Distance is prevalent by surveying the situation and looking at their Virtual Distance Indices, much like the air traffic controller needs to know that there are "x" number of planes in the sky, it's also important they're able to see exactly where Virtual Distance problems are, for example, the exact location of a plane in relation to other planes.

The measurement tools we've described so far (i.e., the Virtual Distance Model and the Virtual Distance Index) give managers the information they need to see the big picture. But to see the detail needed to take specific management action, another tool is needed. That tool is called Virtual Distance Mapping. Mapping Virtual Distance provides a way to see, up close, its effects on collaboration, performance, innovation, and more. Once Virtual Distance has been mapped, then, as you'll see in Chapter 5, managers have what they need to take specific steps to reduce Virtual Distance moving forward.

A fairly straightforward process, Virtual Distance Mapping begins by drawing a diagram of the social network you're interested in. Next, Virtual Distance scores are assigned along the links between individuals in the network. Finally, those paths in the network most critical for success are identified. These steps are shown in Figure 4.1.

Though simple to execute, Virtual Distance Mapping is the most powerful tool a manager or individual has to address Virtual Distance at the source.

To help internalize the Virtual Distance Mapping notion, imagine you're planning a trip. Since every trip requires different kinds of preparation, the map for each will necessarily be different. For instance, if, on the one hand, you're planning a vacation where the goal is to relax and explore your surroundings casually, detailed mapping wouldn't be necessary. In this case, you'd probably let a tour guide handle those or you may just simply stay in one place. On the other hand, if you're planning an important business trip, you have to consider specific dates, locations, meeting times, transportation schedules, transfer or waiting times at airports, and so on. In this case, the trip must be mapped precisely if you're to achieve your goals. This latter scenario

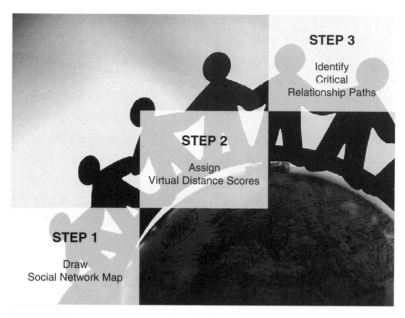

FIGURE 4.1 Steps to Map Virtual Distance

is analogous to Virtual Distance Mapping in that it is detail oriented and impacts time and budget.

Some companies use a social networking process to better understand the organization. For instance, at Intel, Eleanor Wynn developed the Virtuality Index[1] and applied it to social networks in order to better understand the company's social fabric. Now Intel, whose workforce is more than 50% virtual, electronically draws social network diagrams revealing certain aspects of relationships, such as communications activity via e-mail, how many projects a person is assigned to, geographic location, divisional affiliation, and more. However, the software cannot predict how the underlying nature of the relationships between people in a group or team impact organizational outcomes. Virtual Distance Mapping, however, is able to predict this impact, and by doing so, a manager can understand not only the flow of information between individuals, but the *quality* of the links established between them. With this knowledge, collaboration within social networks can be increased.

There are other benefits to mapping Virtual Distance. First, mapping allows a manager to see where Virtual Distance is creating the most risk. By pinpointing where high-stakes projects are the most threatened, it's easier to prioritize target fixes. Remember, not all Virtual Distance is equally detrimental to virtual unity and therefore, fixing Virtual Distance where it has little to no impact is a waste of time. Second, by mapping Virtual Distance, team members have a guide that can be used to track progress. Once the social network is mapped, Virtual Distance levels assigned, and critical paths are identified, one can go back to them over time, to see if the solutions implemented are making a difference. Revisiting the maps also helps one to see how Virtual Distance might be shifting around in various groups and teams. Finally, once people have built Virtual Distance Mapping skills, they're easily transferable to other projects. And if this activity takes hold on a widespread basis, Virtual Distance Mapping can eventually be used in strategic planning and other long-term initiatives to cut off Virtual Distance before it begins to develop.

CASE STUDY: MAPPING VIRTUAL DISTANCE

The China Case

The China Case involves two organizations, a university-based consulting group and a large multinational high-tech company. The people involved are located in three different locations: New Jersey, New York, and Beijing, China.

The first official project meeting took place as a conference call and was led by Joe, the project manager for the university team. The purpose of the call was to introduce everyone involved and agree to a set of steps in order to move the project forward. The call didn't go well. Communication problems, including language barriers as well as mismatched expectations, prevented any meaningful exchange. Joe had to abruptly end the call in frustration and regroup.

Step One: Drawing the Social Network Map   Joe mapped out the people he was working with. This provided him with his first picture of the situation. Joe's initial social network map is depicted in Figure 4.2.

Joe had first met with the New York executive at his high-tech company office when the project was approved. Joe had never met the project manager in Beijing—the person responsible for the day-to-day project tasks and its ultimate success. Joe knew that for the project to do well, Virtual Distance between him and the project manager in

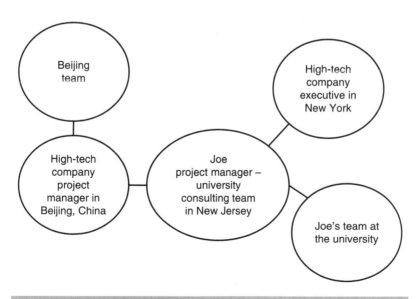

FIGURE 4.2 Joe's Initial Social Network Map

China had to be reduced. So, after a particularly exasperating call, Joe "scored" the different Virtual Distance issues at play.

Step Two: Assigning Virtual Distance Scores   Clearly, *physical distance* between Joe and the Beijing manager was *high*. *Geographic distance* was at a max. *Temporal distance* was extreme, since there were many time zones between them. *Organizational distance* was vast. After all, they worked for different organizations and, in this case, two different industries: high-tech and academia.

And Joe wasn't surprised either that *operational distance* between them was also *high*. *Communications distance* was extensive; both struggled with language differences and the inability to read body language and other cues that normally exist face to face. They simply couldn't reach a sense of "shared understanding" via either phone or e-mail. They were also beset by excessive *multitasking*: This was not the only project on either of their plates, so attention had to be split between this and other work, further weakening their efforts to succeed. On top of that, *distribution asymmetry* posed a problem for Joe because the people at the high-tech company responsible for day-to-day project success were all based in China.

And finally, though not surprisingly, Joe detected *high affinity distance* between him and his Chinese counterpart. There was no way for them to know whether their values were aligned and their communication styles were very different. So *cultural distance* was high. Frustration around communications even translated into an "irrational" sense, on each of their parts, that the other was being difficult, causing further detriments to affinity building. Their troubles also stemmed from *relationship distance*, since they had never worked together before. The weak ties between them, through the executive in New York, were especially weak and therefore made little difference. *Social distance* also contributed to dysfunctional behaviors. Joe thought the formal status of the New York executive would overcome any mismatched expectations about the importance of the project. But that wasn't the case, in part, because *interdependence distance* also impacted them. In the few conversations that Joe was able to understand, it seemed that the project was not in line with the Beijing manager's objectives.

Figure 4.3 below shows Joe's initial pass at the Virtual Distance Map.

Joe realized, after he initially mapped Virtual Distance, that various issues had to be resolved for the project to succeed—especially in the affinity and operational distance corners of the Virtual Distance Model. He knew that in order to do so, he would have to meet with the Chinese team face to face to spark affinity and lower communications distance. So he went to Beijing, taking university team members with him, and met with the project manager and his team both in groups and one on one.

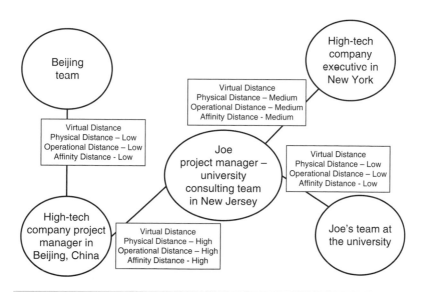

FIGURE 4.3 Joe's Virtual Distance Score Assignments

During his first trip, communications distance broke down despite language barriers. Because the two men were face to face, they were able to establish a rhythm and context to their conversations, which then led to meaningful understanding between them. They were then able to reach consensus on important project issues through better communications and, soon after, established a shared sense of mission.

In addition, Joe learned the Chinese manager hadn't been thoroughly informed about the nature of the project, his role in it, and what was in it for him. When Joe explained what he had discussed with the executive in New York, the Beijing manager better understood how the initiative played into his objectives more directly. They also discovered shared work and personal values, infusing the project with new vitality. Affinity developed and Virtual Distance fell. By simply meeting his counterpart, Joe was able to reduce the Virtual Distance factors that plagued them in their initial conference calls and e-mails.

By the time Joe left China, he felt they'd taken a big step forward. As the weeks passed, much progress was made. Even though language differences still existed, Joe "knew" what the Chinese manager "meant" in his e-mails, and even regular conference calls were positive and successful. The quality of their relationship increased dramatically and, two months later, they'd overseen the completion of the project's first phase. Soon after, together they prepared a presentation for the New York executive and were optimistic they'd get his approval to finish the project.

Reflecting on the experience, Joe realized he could now "rescore" the Virtual Distance between him and the project manager in China.

While Joe knew that *physical distance* would be a constant source of trouble for this global, cross-boundary project, he discovered that physical distance is readily mitigated. Despite high geographic, temporal, and organizational distance throughout the work effort, Joe was able to neutralize the effects by having one face-to-face meeting in the beginning and. afterward, initiating and maintaining strategies (face-to-face meetings, videoconferencing etc.) that built a sense of familiarity between them. This increased trust, helped them both to stay focused on their role and goals, and motivated each of them to help one another.

Operational distance was lowered drastically by the initial face-to-face encounter that drew down *communications distance*, a serious barrier at the outset. Language differences alone, at first, made collaboration extremely difficult. While these issues never completely disappeared, they became inconsequential, and quality relationships were easily established. Later, if an e-mail caused misunderstandings, individuals were more inclined to seek clarification by phone, text messaging, or videoconferencing. It was true that *multitasking* remained high for them both. However, a renewed sense of commitment brought with it a higher priority to this particular project. *Distribution asymmetry* remained high; however, like physical distance, it became less of an issue over time.

Finally, *affinity distance* was significantly reduced, producing an overall decline in Virtual Distance. As was mentioned earlier, Joe and the project manager in Beijing quickly learned that they shared similar values regarding their views of work and success. *Relationship distance*, therefore, basically disappeared between them, and *social distance*, which was once high also dissipated as each of them contributed valuable insights and activities to the work. Formal status differences faded, replaced by mutual respect and an appreciation for each other's contributions. And when they saw how their individual success would be enhanced by each other, *interdependence distance* dropped sharply. As a result of these dynamics, affinity for one another grew.

After this second analysis, Joe redrew his Virtual Distance Map, represented in Figure 4.4.

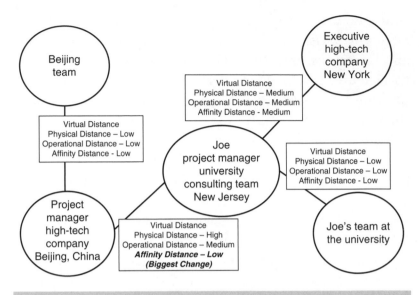

FIGURE 4.4 Joe's Updated Virtual Distance Map at End of Project

But the China case didn't end there. Confident, Joe and the Chinese project manager presented the results of their work to the executive in New York. They were convinced that the work clearly justified moving ahead with a larger initiative, requiring large capital investment and other resource commitments. Much to their dismay, however, the New York executive was unimpressed with their arguments and abruptly killed the project. The two were astonished at the decision. To them, it made no sense whatsoever given that all original goals had been exceeded and they'd shown how a larger project would enhance the company's global operations.

What they hadn't realized was that while they'd closed the gap on their own Virtual Distance, they'd inadvertently ignored the Virtual Distance spreading between themselves and the final decision maker.

Step Three: Identifying Critical Relationship Paths   In unifying virtual teams, we must not only identify the Virtual

Distance along individual links, we also need to isolate and reduce distance along what we call *critical relationship paths*. Critical relationship paths, like critical paths in project management, highlight the people most important to a given project. Obviously, then, it's vital (as Joe learned) that Virtual Distance among those in critical relationship paths be continuously monitored to avoid project delay, or worse, as we've seen, unintended failures.

By identifying and mapping critical relationship paths, managers can focus their Virtual Distance management efforts on those people-based dependencies that have the highest likelihood of impacting project outcomes. The critical relationship path and final Virtual Distance scores for the China case are shown in Figure 4.5.

Virtual Distance Mapping is the way we help companies to "light up" specific locations in a people network where Virtual Distance impedes collaboration and cooperation. After conducting Virtual Distance Mapping sessions, individuals as well as managers see more clearly the bottlenecks in their

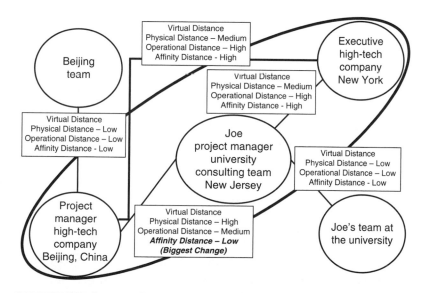

FIGURE 4.5 Critical Relationship Paths in the China Case

organizations. This gives them the picture they need to zero in on and fix problems.

INSTRUCTIONS FOR MAPPING VIRTUAL DISTANCE

Think of a project or work initiative in which you are involved. Begin with you in the center and draw a social network map. Include all the people involved in the project or work initiative either directly (those that you work with one on one) or indirectly (those involved who you think are important but don't necessarily work with on a regular basis).

Remember the China case. Make sure that you include all the organizations and individuals that can influence your project as well as those that come to mind readily. For example, if you work with outsourcing resources, include them in the map along with those that work in your organization.

Important: Do not try to map your entire social network. If you do, you will quickly find that it takes too long. We have seen that as a result, people get frustrated and give up the effort because they try to go too far.

Next, assign Virtual Distance scores along each of the connections. To do this, you need to estimate Virtual Distance between all direct and indirect links. But this process does not have to be precise. It is important, however, that you think through each of the Virtual Distance issues carefully. To help you with this, we have included a Virtual Distance estimation tool in Figure 4.6.

The next step is to look for critical relationship paths. This involves circling those individuals that are most important to the project's success (see Figure 4.4). Remember that there may be more than one critical relationship path, as we saw in the China case. To help you identify critical

FIGURE 4.6 Virtual Distance Estimation Tool

Estimation	Physical Distance	Operational Distance	Affinity Distance
Low	• Same location	• Face-to-face or phone interactions for more than 50% of communications	• Work group or team members usually understand and respect each other's work ethics and values
	• Same time zone	• No technical support problems	• Communication styles among group or team members are highly compatible
	• Same work schedule	• Assigned to one project or work initiatve with little to no deliverable overlap	• Most of the work or group members either knew each other before the start of the initiative or project or knew a lot of the same people
		• Other core group or team members involved in a majority of communications	• Status within the work group or team is based on contribution to the work, not formal titles or affiliations
			• Most work group or team members are working toward the same goals and feel they need to depend on each other

(Continued)

FIGURE 4.6 (Continued)

Estimation	Physical Distance	Operational Distance	Affinity Distance
Medium	• Same country • Within three time zone differences • Similar work schedules	• Face-to-face or phone interactions for 20% to 50% of communications • Intermittent technical support problems • Assigned to two to three projects or work initiatives with some deliverable schedule overlap • Other core group or team members involved in some communications	• Work group or team members sometimes understand and respect each other's work ethics and values • Communications and styles among group or team members are moderately compatible • Some of the work or group members knew each other before the start of the initiative or project or knew some of the same people • Status within the work group or team is sometimes based on contribution to the work and sometimes based on formal titles or affiliations • Some work group or team members at times work toward the same goals and sometimes feel that they need to depend on one another

High	• Different country • More than 3 time zones differences • Different work schedules	• Face-to-face or phone interactions for less than 20% of communications • Regular technical support problems • Assigned to more than three projects or work initiatives with a high level of deliverable schedule overlap • Other core group or team members involved in only a small portion of communications	• Work group or team members do not understand and respect each other's work ethics and values • Communications and styles among group or team members are difficult or hard to understand • Few if any of the team members knew each other or others in common before the start of the initiative or project • Status within the work group or team is based mainly on formal titles or affiliation • Work group or team members do not work toward the same goals and do not feel that they need to depend on one another

FIGURE 4.7 Critical Path Estimation Tool

If you are:	Estimation Guidelines for Critical Relationship Paths (If a "Yes" is checked, then the relationship is likely part of the critical relationship path)	Yes	No
An individual contributor with no management responsibility	• The person has formal authority over you within your company directly or indirectly **OR** • The person has formal or informal authority over you from outside the company—either directly or indirectly		
	• The person controls resources that you need to get your job done		
	• The person controls budget that you need to get the job done		
	• The person is the formal or informal champion of the work initiative or project		
	• The person is an influential customer or user of the work initiative or project output		
	• The group or team member has strong influence over other group or team members		
A manager or leader or a work initiative group or project team, then all of the above apply as well as consideration of those you oversee	• The group or team member has strong influence and/or direct personal relationships with those that you marked as critical, given the guidelines above		

relationship paths, we have included a critical relationship path estimation tool in Figure 4.7.

In conclusion, Virtual Distance Mapping is akin to the headlights on your car—the process shines light on potential dangers that might drive you right off the road. Virtual Distance Mapping is nothing like most of today's virtual team approaches that suggest fixes designed for "industrial age" organizations transported into the virtual workforce. We've seen this fail time and time again. Virtual Distance Mapping provides the road map needed to focus solutions around context-specific virtual work problems, serving up a course that has been missing in virtual team problem solving until now.

With your Virtual Distance Maps in hand, you're ready to build your Virtual Distance Management Plan and execute resolutions that are sure to increase collaboration and enhance virtual workforce unity.

NOTE

1. Katherine M. Chudoba et al., How virtual are we? Measuring virtuality and understanding its impact in a global organization, *Information Systems Journal*, 15 (2005): 279.

~ 5 ~

Managing Virtual Distance

Managing Virtual Distance is a challenging endeavor, but one that results in higher productivity and project success, improved innovation, higher job satisfaction, trust, organizational citizenship, and all those things that create effective teams and keep them that way.

Our data show that when Virtual Distance is managed properly and kept relatively low, positive results skyrocket:

- Innovation behaviors increase by 93 percent.
- Trust improves by 83 percent.
- Job satisfaction is better by 80 percent.
- Role and goal clarity rise by 62 percent.
- On-time, on-budget performance is better by 50 percent.
- Helping behaviors go up by almost 50 percent.

But getting to these results is demanding because each situation requires a different set of strategies and tactics to put teams on the right track to achieve goals. Adding to these difficulties, Virtual Distance usually shifts over time, weighted more toward affinity distance at some points and more toward operational or physical distance at others. And all the factors are linked to boot!

Remember the China case in the previous chapter. Virtual Distance was initially manageable between the executive in New York and the university project manager. At the same time, Virtual Distance factors were high between the two key project managers. Over time, however, lowering affinity distance helped bring those two closer, thereby diminishing other potentially harmful effects. But, in parallel, originally moderate levels of Virtual Distance with the decision maker increased, which ultimately caused the project to be killed.

So when planning for Virtual Distance management, remember that while many Virtual Distance factors may be in play at the same time, it's important to look at both those causing damage in the present as well as those that are likely to pose obstacles in the future.

But how does one go about making sense of all this information and taking appropriate action to solve or mitigate problems? The answer is to develop a Virtual Distance Management Plan (VDMP). The VDMP serves as a way to help decide what actions to take, when, and with whom in order to minimize Virtual Distance. We have developed the Virtual Distance Management Plan template to help focus attention on the most critical issues and it is included here in Figure 5.1.

Once you have gone through Virtual Distance Mapping and have identified the relationships that need the most attention, you are left with two major steps to implement solutions:

Step 1. Establish or reestablish clear goals.

Step 2. Select short-term tactics and long-term strategies.

These areas are shaded in gray in Figure 5.1.

FIGURE 5.1 Virtual Distance Management Plan

Project Goals		*Use **DUMB** Project goals to unify a virtual workforce*			Short-Term Tactics	Long-Term Strategies
Relationship	**Physical Distance**	Geographic				
		Temporal				
		Organizational				
	Operational Distance	Communications Distance				
		Multitasking				
		Readiness				
		Distribution				
	Affinity Distance	Cultural				
		Social				
		Relationship Distance				
		Interdependence Distance				
					Quick Fixes	**Competitive Strategies**
1						
2						
3						
4						
...						

91

ESTABLISH OR REESTABLISH A CLEAR PROJECT GOAL

In our twenty-first-century world it's easy to lose sight of goals because we often get so intensely focused on project due dates and lose perspective about the bigger picture and our place in it. However, if no overarching goal is made clear—one that everyone involved can understand—then the hurried pace of work is likely to pull people away from reaching it. There is an old saying; "If you don't know where you're going, any road will take you there." So how can people overcome physical separation, operational difficulties, and relationship hurdles if everyone is on a different path? Of course, they can't. Therefore, clearly articulating the project goals *before* trying to find ways to solve related problems is a critical first step. Some tips for establishing or reestablishing goals are shown in Figure 5.2.

FIGURE 5.2   Tips for Creating DUMB Goals

When establishing or reestablishing goals for a virtual workforce, it's imperative to know when to be **SMART** and when to be **DUMB**.

a. The term most often used for goal setting is **SMART**, which usually stands for specific, measurable, achievable, realistic, time framed. But when working with people all over the world, who are likely to be segmented into groups that are working on bits and pieces of different parts of any given deliverable, it's almost impossible to ask everyone to work toward the *same* SMART goal because this usually means too many different things to the many varied people involved in distributed work. SMART goals are most effective when applied to subsets of virtual teams.

b. **DUMB** goals, however, are those that everyone in a larger virtual workforce can appreciate as a group as well as at the individual level. **DUMB** goals should invoke self-motivation. And the same

DUMB goals should be repeated often by managers around the world who share responsibility for the end result. Managers need to establish goals for the virtual workforce that are:

i. **D**irect—everyone can **directly** internalize how they themselves are important to the end result.

ii. **U**nderstandable—everyone needs to share the same **understanding** of the goal.

iii. **M**eaningful—the goal has to provide purposeful **meaning** for those involved in the work.

iv. **B**elievable—the goal ultimately has to be something that everyone can **believe** in.

SELECT SHORT-TERM TACTICS AND LONG-TERM STRATEGIES

Some problems can be fixed in the short term (*quick fixes*) and others need to be tackled as a long-term strategy (*competitive strategies*). Managers have more control over quick fixes, even though they might be challenged to execute them, as we discuss later on. Competitive strategies are more difficult to steadily steer because of the changing nature of the work and resources. Ultimately, it is imperative that strong leaders be involved in developing forward-looking plans.

Quick Fixes—Short-Term Tactics to Minimize Virtual Distance

There are four basic quick-fix categories from which to build a custom plan to minimize Virtual Distance. They broadly include:

1. Judicious use of face-to-face meetings
2. Careful coordination of work
3. Ad hoc cross-functional team development
4. Communication improvements

Judicious Use of Face-to-Face Meetings   Face-to-face meetings are the quickest way to overcome a number of pain points that surface as a result of Virtual Distance—especially for geographic distance, communications distance, and cultural distance. Face-to-face meetings are most important when:

- *The project first gets off the ground.* This helps to establish trust and familiarity among the team from the outset.
- *There are major problems that need to be discussed openly.* When misunderstandings or lack of open debate might cause disasters, people need to be in close proximity.
- *Presenting major project deliverables,* especially those that are complex or highly technical—communicating end results should be a coordinated effort.
- *Problems need to be brought to the customer.* This is especially important if the team has missed deadlines that could impact the customer's business.
- *Giving performance reviews and/or other career-related assessments.* Any time feedback might potentially threaten the relationship in a way that is not intended, face-to-face meetings are best.

The biggest barrier to implementing face-to-face meetings is budget restrictions. We haven't met a company yet where managers didn't say they needed more face time but weren't allowed to spend money on travel. But this kind of bottom-line thinking fuels Virtual Distance, so superiors need to be convinced it's worth the cost of bringing people together to ensure a project's success. It's imperative, then, to show, in real dollars, what the return on the travel investment will be.

The justification rests in comparing the estimated expenses against the opportunity cost of *not* acting. According to our data, a 50 percent increase in costs can be expected if Virtual Distance is high. Since face-to-face meetings have a profound effect on all of the Virtual Distance variables, then a project costing a million dollars is likely to cost a million and a half if face-to-face meetings are not added in appropriately.

Consider another costly decision. Say the project outcome is a hoped-for "innovation" of some sort. Our data show that innovative behavior declines by 90 percent when Virtual Distance is high. So a million-dollar effort might have an associated opportunity cost of $900,000 or more! And those are just the financials. They don't even account for what it might cost the company in terms of future competitive advantage.

To track costs more specifically, project managers can take the person's *loaded* cost and multiply that by time wasted as a result of budget deficits preventing face-to-face collaboration when needed. Loaded costs consist of salary plus any variable pay like bonuses as well as the individual's non-payroll benefits, which can be conservatively estimated at 30 percent of salary. For example, if a person's total compensation is $100,000, his or her loaded cost would be $130,000. Based on an average 22 days per month, 8 hours per day, the company spends approximately $514 per day ($64.25/hour) on this individual.

If a lack of face-to-face meetings leads to just one person's wasting five days of his or her time in a given initiative, then it costs the project $2,570 *plus* the expense of fixing the problem, which, for the sake of argument, takes five days of another person's time (at $130,000), costing an additional $2,570. The *opportunity cost* is now at least $5,640. And this estimation is only if *one* person is involved in the problem.

But this is never the case because by definition, Virtual Distance occurs between at least two people—a botched communication has repercussions for *both* the sender and the receiver for example. So our previous opportunity cost doubles and goes to $11,280. And this doesn't include other hidden costs like potential damage done to the company's relationship with its clients or reputation damage if it involves a particularly public project. But let's say there is more than one such incident involving two people. Say there are five such incidents each month and the project is six months long. In that case, the cost of the problem could be an estimated $340,000.

What, then, would it cost to avoid the problem? Well, if the manager were allowed to take ten people, for example, and get them together for three days at the beginning of the project, at an average expense of $4,000 per person, the meeting would cost approximately $40,000. If he/she had to have, perhaps, two more face-to-face meetings with half that number of people at a cost of another $40,000, then the total investment would be $80,000. Is this a justifiable expense if it will save $340,000? Only the company can decide.

Careful Coordination of Work   Diligence around work coordination can rapidly help to minimize temporal distance, communications distance, multitasking, and relationship distance. Each of these factors disturbs the natural ebb and flow of group work.

For example, one telecommunications manager told us that he never schedules a team meeting when it's late at night for his India-based team members because it would be a logistical hardship. To get to a broadband connection, they have to travel long distances. In addition, to be outside at night, in their work locations, is quite dangerous; therefore, he opts to regularly bear the burden of being up late at night so his Indian counterparts can take calls during their normal work hours. By considering "on the ground" realities, managers can raise everyone's comfort level by watching out for those who need the most attention.

Important coordination guidelines include:

- Discuss and get agreement from the team about when to use real-time versus asynchronous communications like e-mail. By doing so, there should be less scheduling difficulties and better expectation management.

- Make sure that turnaround times for any given communication are well understood by all. Does the team expect someone to answer them within a minute? An hour? A day? While obviously there will be variations, in the beginning, don't leave this ambiguous. Establish norms around response time frames.

- Do not use "urgent" on e-mail messages if the work is not due immediately. This causes disruption in work schedules that is not necessary.

- Know your time zones. Memorize time differences between you and your team members. This will create better behavior when it comes to optimizing schedules.

- When confirming meetings in e-mail, always include meeting times in terms of everyone's time zone.

- Rotate meeting times to instill a sense of fairness in the process of scheduling work.

- Understand as a manager that not everyone is gifted with good time management skills. Help team members prioritize work and check in to see how they're handling the workload. This will also help uncover multitasking problems.

Ad Hoc Cross-Functional Team Development To expeditiously solve problems related to organizational distance, interdependence distance, cultural distance, and operational distance, create quasi–organizations or temporary teams made up of representatives from different places or organizations. This helps to quickly build trust among a large virtual workforce.

For example, we spoke with several military personnel about a consolidation of locations that was done using a virtual team structure. A boundary-spanning team was assembled, which included a member of each division involved in the restructuring. Each team member represented the interests of his or her own organization, while at the same time developed a group identity among them. This helped everyone in each location to feel more dependent on one another and bridge values differences, and facilitated cooperative communication among people who initially had trepidations about talking with one another openly.

When forming cross-functional teams to overcome Virtual Distance, consider the following:

- Select members that have a strong knowledge of the organization and good skill sets, and are trusted members in their own communities.

- Involve them regularly in "local" decisions to minimize communication problems and maximize ties to other efforts.

- Respect group input and execute recommendations consistently. Some organizations we have worked with have been initially successful in forming cross-functional teams to overcome Virtual Distance, but then ignore their input. The most successful are those that leverage boundary-spanning teams to overcome major issues.

- Rotate members so that multiple people from each organization have a chance to participate. Like an advisory board, members get the chance to hear about global problems and feel more connected to group goals.

- Make sure to include representatives from all locations. At one pharmaceutical company we worked with, the creation of an advisory council, consisting of managers from each of the company's global operations centers, was important to moving past major Virtual Distance blocks.

Communication Improvements Communication problems strongly influence every aspect of Virtual Distance. They're the most insidious issue in today's global workforce and overcoming them requires a tireless effort by both team members and management.

There is not enough room in this book to detail all the communication practices for the virtual workforce. We could probably have written an entire book on this subject alone. For our purpose here, we focus on the issues that fan communications distance to keep this section a manageable read. We start with context and interpretation recommendations and go from there.

- Share context information whenever possible, including environmental conditions such as the weather, noise levels, office space conditions, or other environmental concepts that are universal.
- Be aware of contextual distinctions between you and others. It helps to bring a conscious awareness to your differences, and this can itself go a long way toward changing behaviors.
- In e-mail or voice exchanges, focus on using words that are easy for everyone to understand.

- Use bullets and outlining as much as possible to keep exchanges simple and avoid misinterpretations.
- When sending instructions, model e-mails after recipes in a cookbook.
- Spell things out if needed, and avoid using acronyms that others might not understand.
- Try as best you can not to read too much meaning into e-mail. This is hard because we do this naturally and unconsciously as human beings. But it's a waste of time because the chances of your understanding the exact same thing the person was thinking when he wrote it are about zero.
- When on calls, listen to every word a person is saying as though your life depended on it. If you thought active listening was hard in face-to-face settings, when you're remote, it's obviously harder.
- Err on the side of formality—don't use sloppy grammar because this is even more difficult to understand and shows little respect for others at work.
- Weigh the trade-offs for different communication modes. Use the face-to-face guidelines above when needed. Phone or videoconference is the best substitute but is not always possible given coordination problems. If the video is low quality or technically unstable, then readiness distance could become a problem.
- Select an e-mail etiquette guide you're comfortable with (many are free and can be obtained on the Internet). Get agreement that everyone will follow these guidelines. This way, norms begin to take root and expectations among all can be better managed.

Short-term tactics are an important first step in managing Virtual Distance and need to be employed constantly. For quick fixes, focus on the four tactics outlined and you are likely to see a spike in performance due to lower Virtual Distance.

In the long run, however, these tactics will only go so far. Seen another way, they are reactions to physical and operational distance as we define it. But in the long run, developing strategies to lower affinity-based issues will have the most sustainable impact on the bottom line and competitive advantage.

Long-Term Strategies to Minimize Virtual Distance

Long-term strategies to minimize Virtual Distance interference need to be championed by committed managers because it takes an investment of time, money, and resources over the long haul. Those who truly internalize a brighter future by advancing development of healthy relationships go on to build winning virtual workforce strategies.

Let's take two very different stories and see if the workforce strategies the leaders chose would have been right for you. In June 2006, Randy Mott took over as the chief information officer (CIO) for Hewlett-Packard (HP). It was widely reported that he felt that distributed work was hurting the information technology (IT) division.[1] So he decreed that everyone had to begin physically coming into one of 25 offices around the world in order to enhance learning and improve efficiencies. In that same month, it was reported that Accenture's strategy was to own no real estate and take advantage of places like airport meeting spaces and client offices to bring their cadre of consultants together. These are completely opposite strategies that were employed to deal with what we now know as Virtual Distance.

But in our data we have examples of how both of these strategies can easily fail if Virtual Distance is not managed into the future. Just one example involved a large insurance organization that, like HP, required people to physically come into the office. And yet, the level of Virtual Distance we found in that organization was just as high as in distributed organizations. The reason was mainly affinity distance caused by a high degree of social distance between different levels within the organization and between the parent and acquired companies. Social distance was closely followed by interdependence distance and communications distance.

By working on fixing Virtual Distance versus focusing in on location specifics per se, there was no need to "decree" anything. As practices changed to address these issues, other problems also faded into the background. Stock price rose, managers felt more at ease, relationships were strengthened and therefore physicality became less of a gating factor to success and innovation.

We do not believe that forcing people into one location every day or working entirely without any home base at all is the optimal solution. Strategies like these, designed to deal with Virtual Distance, are executed randomly and may or may not work, but cost a lot of money to implement and a lot of undue stress on the employees involved in both cases. Instead, we recommend building a workforce that is aware of affinity distance problems and committed to minimizing them.

The following subsections discuss strategies to reduce specific Virtual Distance challenges.

Cultural Distance   To reduce cultural distance:

- *Leaders need to encourage conversations in which people talk to one another about what is important to them.* This is not a one-shot deal, and it requires some initial level of trust.

- *Share experiences around hobbies, children, favorite books and movies, and so on, as you feel comfortable.* Do not force this discussion because it would come across to others as disingenuous, which might reflect a false image of you.

- *Respect one another's communication styles.* When possible, try to build some of other's styles into your own, making it easier for them to understand you.

- *Do not assume that everyone is like you—which is our default state of mind.* People are very different, whether they sit across the hall or across the ocean. These differences are what ultimately make people curious about one another. Don't let that curiosity fade because of electronic walls.

Social Distance To reduce social distance:

- *Shine a light on other people's accomplishments.* Far-flung resources or those who stay to themselves often end up a bit disadvantaged when it comes to being recognized, so it is important that leaders maintain vigilance over making sure these individuals are given their fair share of authentic and public praise.

- *Develop traditions around recognizing people's contributions.* Rewards and recognition can be financial as well as nonfinancial; for example, when someone helps out a fellow team member, create a "good Samaritan" award and celebrate together either online or in person as part of a consistent routine.

- *Recognize unsung heroes.* We hear stories all the time about "firefighters"—those who come in on a moment's notice and seem to save everything all by themselves. While these people are clearly important contributors to the team, many feel that their day-to-day, uninterrupted work, which has taken the team ahead to that point, often goes unnoticed.

- *Use each scheduled project meeting to showcase team members.* Make someone the "star" for an hour and ask her to tell the group a bit about herself. This helps across the entire affinity distance spectrum.

Relationship Distance   To reduce relationship distance:

- *Seed teams with people who know each other or know some of the same people.* Even if just a few of the many distributed resources have weak ties, strong relationships are more likely to develop.
- *Encourage social networking among team members.* For example, encourage people within the team to share contact information in much the same way LinkedIn or Facebook works.
- *Ensure that team member relationships are used as input to resource selection for future projects.* This will build to the point where launching teams with low relationship distance is possible.

Interdependence Distance   To reduce interdependence distance:

- *Develop DUMB (direct, understandable, meaningful, believable) goals* (Figure 5.2). It is important up front to ensure that everyone can understand how and why they are important to a larger mission.
- *Reiterate interdependencies among team members.* Managers should make it a part of their regular agendas to restate goals and select examples of how working together furthers everyone's interests in the project.
- *Develop reward programs that include incentives for distributed people to work together.* This last recommendation is tricky because reporting structures and performance appraisal systems may not be set up to do this easily but it is a must-have if interdependence is to be established in a way that is meaningful.

Long-term strategies, by definition, take time to develop and implement. But many of our organizational cultures have become "just-in-time" oriented. However, if companies are to reach a state of competitive advantage in the future, they must better manage their virtual workforces— whether they are in-house employees or external partners like outsourcing resources.

And it's here that we move into a deeper discussion about teams, leadership, innovation, technology, and software, as these are the most important challenges to uniting the virtual workforce.

NOTE

1. Randy Mott, For the H-P Way, a Slap in the Face, *Mercury Sun Times* (June 5th, 2006), http://blogs.zdnet.com.

Part Two

HIGH-IMPACT VIRTUAL
DISTANCE STRATEGIES

~ 6 ~

Redefining Teams

Up to now, we've categorized members of the virtual workforce as belonging to one team or another. That's because, as a corporate society, we've been using this terminology for decades. Teamwork—or that notion, anyway—has actually been around much longer. And even in our global age, when the nature of work over the past decade has changed in every imaginable way, the word *team* is still used to describe basically any collection of resources that loosely work together around a common goal.

But does this still make sense? We don't think so entirely. In fact, the word *team* can be a misnomer and, worse, summon up knee-jerk behaviors that further spread Virtual Distance. As we've learned in the previous sections, this can be quite costly. So we turn our attention to teams and explore why and how this idea should be modified to better face the Digital Age.

A BRIEF HISTORY OF TEAMS

Even before the Industrial Age, work was done by groups gathered as apprentices under the tutelage of master craftsmen. These groups can be traced as far back as the twelfth century and were called *guilds*.

Together with mutual aid, the 'honour' of the craft defined the purpose for which guilds existed. There was a sense of pride in the "*misterium artis*," in the special technique and skill known only to oneself and one's colleagues, and in the excellence of the finished article. Artefacts must be "loyal." To be a skilled craftsman was to occupy and fulfill a recognized role, an officium (lit. duty), with its own dignity.[1]

Guild members were bonded together by a sense of individual pride as well as honor for the group as a whole. Guilds gave way to other kinds of unified organizations and evolved into professional societies and trade unions. And while the number of unions has declined in recent times, the part they played in establishing roles and affinity among specialists who considered themselves peers was an important one.

More recently, during the early twentieth century, Kurt Lewin, a renowned psychologist, made famous the concept of group dynamics.[2] He showed that group motivation was rooted in a shared sense of interdependence around tasks as well as fate—future success or survival. This discovery further fueled the team discussion. Around the same time, Abraham Maslow developed the *Needs Hierarchy Theory*,[3] which described an individual's motivational structure. Groups were an important part of this model. Right above physiological and safety needs were social needs, which included the necessity to have friends and be accepted by other people. According to Maslow, this then led to the desire for esteem, derived from one's self-respect as well as the approval of others. He argued that if these group needs were not satisfied, both the individual and organization would suffer. These theories, along with others, like Elton Mayo's evidence about how productivity in groups improved when they knew someone was paying attention, provided a deep well of research that coagulated into a unifying idea about groups, commonly referred to today as *teams*.

An entire industry sprung up around teamwork. Many of us recall going to team training. This sometimes included watching videos starring figures such as Vince Lombardi, the famed former coach of the Green Bay Packers, showing why teamwork was so important. Together in a room, we watched in slow motion as the football players drove hard down the field to score the winning touchdown. As the film rolled on, full of emotionally charged effort, hardships, and victorious celebrations, the engaging voice of the narrator reminded us that there is "no 'I' in t-e-a-m-s." Who could forget it? And when the video was over, everyone felt a renewed sense of appreciation for one another.

Team compensation also surfaced as an important financial motivator. Variable pay structures were built to support group work. Many large human resources consultancies launched entire practices specializing in team compensation. Nonfinancial as well as financial bonuses were, and still are, given based on both individual and team performance. One of the most pervasive team reward systems was designed for sales. In these plans, a large portion of commissions or bonuses is paid for individual performance. But, typically, there's also some percentage paid for group quota achievement. Salespeople are notorious for acting in their self-interest, but they often feel "pressure" to perform on behalf of the team as well. When they succeed and work well with others, they're often promoted to management positions and beyond. Many C-level executives have a history in sales, in part, because they did well contributing to the team.

But for corporate departments other than sales, like manufacturing and production, natural groups, designed around revenue contribution, were harder to form. That changed when teamwork models, most commonly built on quality objectives, began to surface. By 1972, five million workers belonged to quality circles (QCs) in Japan.[4] Soon after, many American companies followed suit implementing corporate-wide quality initiatives. Today, Six

Sigma is a quality standard used throughout many corporations worldwide. This approach depends on teams achieving excellence.

It wasn't just operations and production departments that were changed by the concept of teams. In 2000, Jean Pierre Garnier, the chief executive officer (CEO) of Glaxo-SmithKline, gave a talk at the British-American Business Association about his use of teams to improve innovation. Garnier described the reshaping of research and development (R&D) at the giant pharmaceutical company. Scientists were put into "start-up"-like groups, each of which had its own CEO. They were given free rein to go after finding new drug compounds. The goal was to create a "competitive spirit" and drive members using common goals designed to benefit the group. Across most industries, team formations sprang up throughout the enterprise and creative managers found appropriate rallying points around which to motivate them.

TODAY'S WORKPLACE

As a result of forces that gathered quite recently, today's organizations are more fragmented than ever before. Unlike the "closed" organizations in which teams were initially formed, the boundaries of companies are not well defined. As the last millennium moved into its final decade, C. K. Prahalad and Gary Hamel popularized the idea of "core competencies," which led to the splintering off of many departments considered organizationally superfluous. Core competencies were organizational-specific strengths defined as "an area of specialized expertise that is the result of harmonizing complex streams of technology and work activity."[5] As an aside, note the emphasis here on task and process, reminiscent of Frederick Taylor's model from a century ago. They espoused that companies rid themselves of any part of the business that didn't directly support the company's core strength.

At the same time, anxiety began to grow around the potential "Y2K" problem. The Y2K bug was widely anticipated to wipe out computer systems around the world. Most feared that when the calendar turned over to 2000, the billions of lines of code running everything from power plants to credit card processing wouldn't recognize the "000" in the date and therefore terminate in an error, bringing everything to a halt. American Express, for example, realized in the mid-1980s that this might cause a problem, and had been working on repairing all the code for more than 15 years prior to the event. But most organizations waited until the late 1990s to focus in on fixing this potential issue. Programmers and systems engineers were hard to find, and there weren't enough to fill the insatiable need to repair software systems worldwide. So many corporations, that had historically relied solely on "in-house" talent to work for their highly valued information systems, reached outside the company walls to find qualified talent to help. This began what is now a common practice: hiring low-cost resources for what is considered to be "mundane" work.

These two catalysts—a focus on core competencies and the race to fix potentially devastating computer bugs— caused massive workforce change that led to the corporate structures we now think of as commonplace. Many companies began to shed whole divisions to (1) center internal resources on specialties and (2) move high-volume, low-value work, like fixing code, outside traditional company boundaries. In many cases, both strategies resulted in more work being sent not only out but also commonly offshore into other countries, where labor was much cheaper than in the United States. Now, of course, outsourcing is one of the mainstream strategies used to lower costs.

The immediate cost savings these changes yielded were irresistible to company executives interested in elevating stock price and profits. So as the twenty-first century dawned, information technology (IT) and operations outsourcing soared. Around the same time, another kind of corporate dilution ideal was becoming popular. Harvard professor and author Henry Chesbrough introduced the notion of "open innovation,"[6] a way to break apart innovation in new product development. It was centered on the idea that technology advancements had created the opportunity for organizations to reach beyond their time-honored borders and look outside for creative resources and, ultimately, profits. Specifically, Chesbrough described *open innovation* to mean that "valuable ideas can come from inside or outside the company and can go to market from inside or outside the company as well. This approach places external ideas and external paths to market on the same level of importance as that reserved for internal ideas and paths to market. . . . " This idea soon won the hearts and minds of many Fortune 500 CEOs. Companies saw that they could tap expertise around the world. Open innovation led to even larger increases in workforce development outside the company and to partnerships that, up until then, wouldn't have been considered. Competitors joined forces in what was, and still is, hailed as open relationships, where information is shared freely and resulting ideas and inspiration leads to new products and services that find their way to bottom–line boosts. In the open innovation strategy, just like core competency and outsourcing, corporate walls were torn down in favor of an unbounded environment.

This trend toward disaggregation in every part of the organization was accompanied by a surge in the use of mobile technologies and information and communication technology (ICT). Businesses realized that not only could they cut costs and increase the possibility of innovation investment returns, but productivity also could be improved by leveraging technology and high-speed communications. Personal digital assistants (PDAs), which included Blackberries and other personal productivity devices, became commonplace at the start of the century; people were equipped with everything they needed to work from anywhere at any time, which, as we've described, contributed to the formation of the virtual workforce—both inside and outside the corporation.

But one of the detriments of this limitless, "always-on" structure is that it's difficult for any one individual inside of it to imagine himself attached to a shared goal. With all of the segmentation within functions, processes, work streams, and especially relationships, it's not always possible for any one objective to be internalized by everyone involved in getting the work done. And when that's the case, it becomes a major problem to develop what Lewin called a *shared fate,* to motivate groups to work as teams.

The elimination of huge chunks of corporate infrastructure in almost all departments, and the vast virtualization of the workforce across a global spectrum, has changed the nature of work in profound ways that impact us at a personal level. Human resources are now spread out in every way, people spend more time with their computers than they do with each other, and communications are, for the most part, filtered through technology channels.

The underlying structures that made teams work the way they did have been widely obliterated. The new state of work creates constant disruptions to "normal" group dynamics. With so much dispersion, it's difficult to imagine how any one group could be defined, even loosely, as a "team" in the way that we thought of teams in the past. And the use of *teams* as a metaphor for virtual work groups is, in many cases, doing more harm than good.

In traditional teamwork, strong emotions about a larger purpose and a clear sense of interdependence motivate members to act. But if that's not the case, and companies are still using this idea as a way to build motivation, then the effort may turn out to be a waste of time or, even worse, create expectations that are impossible for many to achieve. Recall that as far back as when guilds were predominant, people were motivated to work together by a "calling" of sorts—in that case, honor and pride. Lewin's group dynamics were driven in large part by feelings of close links that manifested as a visceral sense to shape a positive and shared future. Working together on tasks, those in the group felt that goals could be realized. Maslow knew that without socially satisfying interactions, a person's motivation to perform would fall off. And Mayo, who poked a huge hole in closely held dogmatic beliefs about the person as a machine, proved that people as a group perform much better when there is a feeling that others care for them as being more than a cog in a wheel.

However, it is no longer the case that virtual workers build emotional ties to one another in the ways that people have done for centuries. The loose organizations of the Digital Age are not usually built for this purpose. If anything, individuals en masse have become more like the specialists of the guild era, only there are no master craftsmen in the lead, and there are millions scattered around the world, leaving a gigantic schism between individual performance criteria and personal motivation to achieve collective goals. And unlike the low or unskilled workers of Taylor's era, today's professionals are highly trained. Many expect open communication instead of strictly controlled information streams espoused by the father of bureaucratic organizations.

So as we look at organizational resources today, we must ask ourselves if we can really say that the workforce operates in teams, virtual or otherwise. Are people structured as closely linked groups who, as a whole, are motivated by deeply emotional and shared beliefs centered on a common purpose? For many, the answer is no. Splintered organizational structures and isolated work efforts often prevent teams, as we have come to understand them, from forming. And the disconnects that exist, between habitually thinking of ourselves as teams and the disconnected reality, has led to a resurgent scramble to find solutions for how to best manage what are commonly called *virtual teams.*

But after researching much of the literature and popular books on the subject of virtual teams, it has become evident that issues framed as "team dysfunction" in today's mobile and highly dispersed workforce, are not really that at all. Our teams are not really dysfunctional. We are simply not really teams. Therefore, it's the classification system and the associated metrics that go along with it that are, in fact, dysfunctional. The problems among today's vast global professional majorities are much more profound than those described in the volumes on this subject; the problems today are symptoms of a much bigger problem—that of a fundamental structural vacuum created by a lack of an organizing principle formulated around groups in this new age.

At the individual level, the absence of any tangible scaffolding on which to build shared identities and goals has created a black hole for many of today's workers in need of some sort of unifying and meaningful structure that fits in with the kind of work they do and the lives they lead. Without it, behaviors are falsely identified as team problems. But the fact of the matter is that, like all human beings, over time, there is a need to feel as though one is part of something bigger—and this remains elusive and unfulfilled in the group known today as the *virtual workforce.*

But if it's not realistic to use the image of a team to develop the inspired motivation needed to reach peak performance, what, then, might replace it? We believe the answer rests in a new form that we call *virtual ensembles.*

VIRTUAL ENSEMBLES

There are many kinds of assemblages that occur naturally and in work-related activities that don't form as a team per se but nonetheless accomplish group goals. In the wild kingdom, for example, zebras are born with what appear to be senseless random patterns of stripes. As single animals, they spend their time grazing and looking for food. However, each unique zebra serves a greater good. Under attack, a single zebra couldn't survive against the ferocity and strength of a hungry lion. However, when they come together by the hundreds to form what looks to the attacker like one gigantic animal, they ward off fatal attacks. The interloper flees because an animal of such seemingly enormous size would surely eat them for lunch. The zebras live as both individuals and herd members, depending on the situation and their exposure to risk or vulnerability at any given time.

An example of how this kind of temporary group formation happens among workers is in cockpit crews. Scheduling crews to pilot a large plane is complicated. The physical whereabouts, flying time, and availability of potential crew members has to be considered, as well as their special skills. So when a crew is selected to get the plane to its destination, they may have never worked together before. But as soon as they enter that small space, each of them knows they are closely linked to a common goal: to get the plane to its destination safely. There is, of course, great risk to each of them if they don't, and not just for the obvious reason—to avoid a crash. It's also because their future careers depend, in part, on how each performs in the presence of another. So, during the flight, they cooperate for these reasons and more. When the final destination is reached, they leave the plane and go back to their individual lives. They spend time apart sharpening skills and acquiring new learning. And the cycle of getting together, flying planes, going back to home base, and so forth continues throughout their career. Over time, some begin to work with the same individuals repeatedly. In these cases, stronger relationships can form, which leads to deeper trust and camaraderie. Friendships outside of the workspace develop. But those that have no reason or desire to build these kinds of relationships don't have to—they are not forced to feel as though they should, due to an artificial organizational structure that assumes this kind of bonding.

Many in today's Digital Age work in one context and join with different people in another. At times, they might be alone in their home or go to an office where they work at a desk or cubicle. At different times, they gather with others, either face to face or electronically. When those interactions end, they go back to their original context, set apart from the group.

This cycle of gathering, going away and working locally and/or alone, and then regrouping is akin to the zebra in the wild or the pilot in a cockpit crew. It's also very much like jazz ensembles, where musicians learn on their own but exercise their unique talents in a group. Musicians are much like Digital Age professionals, too, in that they both have a kind of solitary "relationship" with their work. Musicians spend time with their instruments, as professional work-force members do with their computers and collaboration tools. So there's also a sense of seclusion even when either is physically among others while working.

They are similar in other respects as well. During live performances, ensembles come together in a way that's coordinated and timely. Each member has to be in sync with the others, or else the music won't sound melodious. They are joined in a common goal—in this case, to inspire, soothe, motivate, or even perplex. In any event, they can reach their shared goal only by operating together seamlessly. Members of virtual projects also have to come together and perform. Each has to contribute his or her share of the work in a timely manner and establish harmonious communications with others to achieve goals.

Ensembles meet mainly for three reasons. First, they gather to create new kinds of music. This is often done through improvisational sessions, during which each of the members experiments with an idea he or she has usually thought of beforehand. These get-togethers are called jam sessions. (Some organizations even use the term *jam sessions* to describe online meetings.) Second, musicians get together to rehearse or fix problems in a piece. These can be thought of as "workout" sessions, where members work out difficulties, practice together, and hone group efforts. Finally, they get together to perform. The ultimate satisfaction for many comes in the audience's appreciation for their work.

Virtual workforce members get together for many of the same reasons. First, they get together to innovate, whether it is to invent a new product or to create project plans. Second, virtual group members get together to work out problems. During status meetings and at other times during the work initiative, members join to overcome obstacles. And third, virtual groups come together to produce a final deliverable: a product, service, or software application.

In many respects, members of the virtual workforce are much like those of ensembles. Recontextualizing the notion of a group—why it's formed, when it's important for members to be together, and how to develop common goals that make sense—is an important way to shake off the unconscious denial of today's changed workforce. When one is able to see something in a different light, he or she often gets ideas about how to improve or change it altogether. To get a better sense of this, let's look at a way to assess groups based on ensemble models. A comparison chart is shown in Figure 6.1.

In summary, the structures in which people work have changed dramatically in a very short period of time. Management principles that encourage companies to disaggregate the work as well as the rising influence of technology that separates people from one another and allows them to connect anywhere at any time have come together to

FIGURE 6.1 Ensembles and Virtual Workforce

Ensembles	Virtual Workforce
Is the piece technically well executed?	Is the project on time, on budget, and of high quality?
Does it exploit a variety of elements of music (i.e., rhythm, harmony, melody, texture/timbre)?	Does the project make use of all members' skills and talents maximizing innovation and problem solving?
Is the chief attraction not the music but the words?	Is the chief attraction not the tasks but the goals and relationships?
Are the elements of the work highly integrated so that each supports the other's function?	Are the members working together, and are they appropriately integrated into the work effort?
Does the piece appeal on a variety of levels—intellectual, emotional, spiritual?	Does the project meet the many needs of workforce members, customers, company, other constituencies?
Is there a feeling of "musicality" about it?	Have team members established a good rapport and rhythm, leading to project successes?
Is there satisfying formal organization to the way the gestures are presented and developed?	Do members enjoy their roles and do others enjoy working with them?
Is there a good balance between familiarity and variety, appropriate for the length of the piece?	Is there a good balance between innovative solutions and known solutions to similar kinds of problems?
After having been listened to many times, does the piece still have appeal that is based on some new revelations rather than solely on comfortable familiarity?	After having worked together on different projects, are members still inspired to find new ways to approach problems, or has the group settled into routines that stifle innovation or problem solving?
Do you feel positively stimulated, better, richer, fuller, or improved in some way for having heard the piece?	Are the company and the individual members better off as a result of the group's efforts?

create a workforce in which the members are no longer necessarily tied to each other through organizational attachments or workplace norms. Therefore, many of the organizing philosophies used to motivate, evaluate, and reward individuals have also changed. However, our work practices and mental models about what encourages people to cooperate have not kept up. While there remain some people who might be thought of as working in traditional teams—those who are permanently assigned to one group, work together in the same place, train together, and work toward clearly articulated and common goals—the vast majority of the virtual workforce do not function in this way.

There are structures, however, in which people can see themselves as a group without the ties that bind teams together. We have termed these *virtual ensembles* and used the metaphor of musical ensembles as a way to frame the discussion. Based on what makes an ensemble successful, we can begin to craft metrics that better reflect competencies and requirements for the virtual workforce member in the Digital Age.

NOTES

1. Antony Black, *Guilds and Civil Society in European Political Thought: From the Twelfth Century to the Present* (London: Methuen, 1984), 14.

2. D. Harrington-Mackin, *The Team Building Tool Kit: Tips, Tactics, and Rules for Effective Workplace Teams* (New York: AMACOM, 1994).

3. A. H. Maslov, A Theory of Human Motivation, *Psychological Review* 50 (1943):370-96.

4. D. Harrington-Mackin, *The Team Building Tool Kit: Tips, Tactics, and Rules for Effective Workplace Teams* (New York: AMACOM, 1994).

5. C. K. Prahalad and Gary Hamel, *The Core Competence of the Corporation* (Cambridge, MA: Harvard Business Review, 1990).

6. Henry Chesbrough, *Open Innovation: The New Imperative for Creating and Profiting from Technology* (Cambridge, MA: Harvard Business School Press, 2003) 43.

~7~

Ambassadorial Leadership

In the last chapter, we described a way to reimagine teams as virtual ensembles and how, by doing so, it's likely that we can significantly increase performance and inject a renewed energy and sense of well-being to those individuals cast as the virtual workforce. In much the same way as teams, the notion of leadership needs to be reimagined as well. First, we consider some of the current views of leadership.

TRANSACTIONAL LEADERSHIP

Perhaps the most traditional view of leadership is that of a manager: one who monitors, controls, and, more importantly, rewards desired behavior and punishes undesired behavior. This kind of leadership views the relationship with followers as a series of transactions. I will reward you with something you want (e.g., money) if you do what I ask you to do. Sometimes called *transactional leadership*, this approach still prevails. But most scholars make a big distinction between management and leadership. Even though transactional leadership can be effective, most see leadership as something more than a series of transactions. True

leadership involves an emotional connection with followers, which can be created differently depending on the style
of leadership. Two views of leadership that emphasize this
emotional connection are charismatic leadership and transformational leadership.

CHARISMATIC LEADERSHIP

Charismatic leaders are people who can make the emotional connection. George Washington, Napoleon, Mao
Tse Tung, and many other historical figures exemplify what
many people think of as leaders: heroic and charismatic figures who, by virtue of their personal qualities, are able to
transform a nation. Charismatic leaders can also appear in
the business world, and, indeed, there has been a fair amount
of scholarship devoted to charismatic leadership. Certainly,
some of the positive aspects of charismatic leadership, such
as inspiring high levels of commitment, can be an asset. But
the consensus on charismatic leadership is that it's a mixed
bag. Although such leaders can attract incredibly devoted
followers, they also tend to be divisive and can even be destructive, as the history of the twentieth century has shown
us. Charismatic leaders depend on a strong emotional connection with their followers, which in virtual organizations
can be difficult to create and sustain over time. It's not clear
whether charismatic leadership is possible or even relevant
in the virtual enterprise.

TRANSFORMATIONAL LEADERSHIP[1]

One of the most popular models of leadership consid-
ers the behaviors that can transform people and organizations. Transformational leadership includes four kinds of
behavior:

1. *Idealized influence* refers to actions that demonstrate vision, values, and beliefs and creates a sense of identification with the leader among followers.

2. *Individualized consideration* involves coaching and encouraging and also promoting each individual's belief that they can be successful.

3. *Inspirational motivation* involves creating a clear and appealing vision and serving as a model for desired behavior.

4. *Intellectual stimulation* involves making the team aware of problems and bringing new ideas so that followers become engaged in finding solutions.

Transformational leaders also create an emotional connection with their followers so that their behaviors contribute to followers' sense of ownership and commitment to the team's goals and tasks. One of the benefits of transformational leadership is that it can get people to transcend their own self-interests. Getting people to share their expertise, help other people with problems, and generally be good corporate citizens is one outcome of effective transformational leadership. In fact, people who study leadership and team behavior spend a fair amount of time looking at organizational citizenship behavior (OCB) because it is one of the keys to great team performance. You also might recall that Virtual Distance has a negative influence on OCB. One reason might be that transformational leadership behaviors do not work as well in a virtual organization.

Transactional, charismatic, and transformational views of leadership were developed before the Digital Age, when collocation was the norm and organizations and teams tended to be more culturally homogeneous. Are these models of leadership completely obsolete? Of course they're not. Leaders still have to find a way to inspire and motivate people, get commitment, and manage the work. But accomplishing this with a globally distributed, digitally connected organization requires another view of the leader that we call the *ambassadorial leader*.

Before we describe this new model, listen to what a senior executive from Aventis has to say about virtual work and trying to gather the leadership team together:

> What's the difference (between being live or on the phone)? When people were there, sitting around a table like this, they were really more engaged and were required to be more engaged in the conversation—whether they wanted to be or not. I was in France at a time we were having one of our management meetings in Paris, so I joined the team on the videoconference from another manager's office. And he is there doing his e-mail, not paying attention—he has to be there but he's not listening. You really don't get the full benefit of people's not just concentration but their input—but feeling like they're part of the leadership team. It's one of those "I have to be here because I am required to be here, but I don't want to be here because I don't really feel connected to the discussion." And this was a big issue for us, especially when I had to deal with serious human resources issues and the leadership was not engaged.

Leading globally distributed teams presents many challenges created by Virtual Distance. Physical distance makes it difficult for leaders to interact with followers. Operational distance presents significant obstacles to leaders trying to communicate a vision, clarify roles, and monitor progress. Finally, affinity distance can lower trust and adversely impact an individual's commitment—necessary ingredients for high performance. Successful leaders balance concern for people against reaching objectives while driving innovation and change efforts forward. But Virtual Distance can detract or even destroy these efforts. Some examples of how this happens are shown in Figure 7.1.

Managers in the highly controlled companies of the pre-Digital Age had overriding power and influence as well as

FIGURE 7.1 Virtual Distance Impacts on Leader Efforts

Virtual Distance Factor	Leader Efforts		
	Task/Goal Accomplishment	Concern for People and Relationships	Innovation and Change
Physical distance	Monitoring progress is difficult.	Difficult to build more than a transactional relationship and establish trust.	Coordinating collaborative efforts are difficult with multiple organizations.
Operational distance	Technology and software can impede progress.	Individual consideration is hard for the leader to express without regular face-to-face interactions.	Multiple projects and divided attention impede innovative behavior.
Affinity distance	Encouraging commitment and effectively motivating followers to achieve goals is stymied.	Cultural differences create misunderstandings; social distances in the form of leader-follower distance in conjunction with the other Virtual Distance pieces is amplified.	Risk taking is hampered due to lower levels of trust, which leads to less innovative behavior and problem solving among followers.

the ability to oversee much of the actual day-to-day work, gaining commitment from followers either through personal traits such as likeability and charisma or from harsher approaches such as threats and punishments. Achieving results was more straightforward because there was little in the way of Virtual Distance. Followers knew exactly what was happening to the rest of the group by watching the leader in action. But virtual workforces susceptible to high levels of Virtual Distance present a very different picture. Each element of the Virtual Distance Model creates different challenges for new-millennium leaders.

PHYSICAL DISTANCE AND LEADERSHIP

Physical distance means that real separation in the form of space, time, and organizational affiliation makes it difficult for leaders to do some of the things that they took for granted with collocated teams and organizations. Leaders who used the technique of "management by walking around," for example, no longer have this available to them. The conversations and coaching sessions in the lunchroom and hallways that happened by chance are difficult to replicate when some or all of the followers are not easily physically accessible. Inspiring followers when they're all together to renew commitment to work initiatives is almost impossible on a regular basis when time zones deter leaders from being able to talk to an entire group simultaneously. Physical distance poses a unique challenge in that leaders have to be able to span the boundaries created by geographic, temporal, and organizational separation. When there are big differences, the leader has to find a solution that works and that everyone thinks is fair.

OPERATIONAL DISTANCE AND LEADERSHIP

Technology is great. We can communicate across vast distances, send and receive documents, and even see one another live. But anyone who's been there can tell you there's a big difference between meeting face to face and meeting via teleconference or video conference. The lowered social presence created by remote conferencing leads to lower levels of arousal and engagement. On top of that, interruptions from instant messaging, cell phones, and unexpected visits create distractions that make it difficult to keep the team in focus.

The mode of communication, the multiple tasks and projects, and the size and distribution of the team can make it difficult to lead effectively. Leading across operational distance requires an understanding of the limitations of the technology and how the distribution of the group can impact interactions.

AFFINITY DISTANCE AND LEADERSHIP

Affinity distance arises from several sources and is especially difficult for leaders. In an interview with the chief information officer (CIO) of a major international bank, we heard how significant challenges brought on by cultural distance and other affinity factors posed challenges for him:

> Even the most basic thing, how to develop software, is vastly different in various cultures. Whereas you have in the States a kind of entrepreneurial type mentality, but kind of also a little bit of the seat of the pants, very aggressive, not as formal process-wise. Whereas in some other regions and cultures, the precision around project management is extremely important—dotting all the I's, crossing the T's, thinking everything through. Now what you have is a situation where these teams are being mixed, and right away you have this difference. And so what it takes is a lot of work and time, but you have to figure out a way to take the best of both cultures and processes and come up with something that's a hybrid that will take some adapting to by both, but is something that they can aspire to. So the challenge is really beyond a process thing because that's a cultural

thing, that's a values thing. And so as you create these virtual teams in the workforce, you have to then deal with these differences at a much higher level. And the challenge for management and leadership is how to bring that together and really take the best practices out of those different cultures and processes and make it all work together, and that's a big challenge. And I don't think it happens overnight. It's something that happens over time.

Affinity distance is the most powerful force in determining whether a team or organization will be able to work together virtually. Understanding how to manage affinity distance requires an appreciation for, and an openness to, differences in cultural values, language, and communication styles.

It takes a different kind of leader to manage an organization or team when Virtual Distance is high. We call this new kind of leadership *ambassadorial leadership*.

THE LEADER AS AMBASSADOR

The ambassadorial leader is a boundary spanner. Like an ambassador, the leader must span geographic, cultural, and organizational boundaries and foster trusting relationships among disparate groups of people. What are the hallmarks of an effective ambassadorial leader? First, effective leaders understand how Virtual Distance can hamper relationships and take steps to mitigate the factors. Specific behaviors for ambassadorial leaders include the following:

- *Communication clarity.* Functional, cultural, and geographic differences sometimes muddy the waters and lead to misunderstandings of goals, objectives, and responsibilities. Being able to clearly articulate the vision for a project or organization and communicate it in a way that everyone understands clearly is essential for all leaders, but it's especially important for virtual workforce members who are distributed in multiple locations and sometimes have little else in common than being on the team.

- *Cultural sensitivity.* Sensitivity and openness to other cultures are key elements of an ambassadorial leader. The leader also communicates this sensitivity and openness to followers.

- *Context sensitivity.* Ambassadorial leaders are hyper-vigilant about understanding context in terms of the individual team member and the group as a whole. Ambassadorial leaders know the physical surroundings in which an individual works as well as the mental model or worldview that person holds. In managing the group, ambassadorial leaders help others to understand each other's contexts and ensure that context awareness is a priority among all group members.

- *Boundary spanning.* Ambassadorial leaders help virtual workforce members to build relationships so that the group can form a collective identity. This kind of activity involves spanning multiple boundaries like different locations as well as organizations in which any given individual might work. Another important boundary-spanning activity for the ambassadorial leader is building relationships between members and other teams or organizations. As we've noted throughout, virtual workforce members don't feel as though they belong to any given organization therefore forming a collective identity and ensuring this identity can also be seen by others is an important mission of the ambassadorial leader.

- *Advocacy.* Distributed teams can often go underappreciated because they're not physically close to the power centers and because they're often spread not only geographically but functionally. Ambassadorial leaders represent the team to senior management and make sure that the team and its members are recognized, celebrated and rewarded.

- *Shared leadership.* A key characteristic of an ambassadorial leader is the capacity to share leadership. Much like an ambassador has attachés, a leader has team members in each location who serve a leadership role. In order for this to work, leaders have to be willing to share sensitive information and trust the attachés to make decisions.

- *Leader intent.* To build an effective cadre of attachés Ambassadorial Leaders need to communicate their vision and feelings about strategy and tactics to those that will share leader responsibilities. Ambassadorial Leaders understand that it's important to develop a kinship with attachés; one that enables the attaché to carry forth the vision of the leader. This can be done through providing guidance around their intentions, which are not as prescriptive as they are descriptive of a larger goal. When the leader is absent or purposefully unavailable, then it's up to the attaché to represent the leader's intent, which can be communicated and set forth by the attaché.

Do ambassadorial leaders exist? We not only think so, we know one. Karan Sorenson, a senior vice president at Johnson & Johnson, exemplifies all of the qualities of an effective ambassadorial leader.

CASE STUDY: GLOBAL IT AT J&J

Johnson & Johnson is one of the world's most recognizable brands. J&J is proud of its decentralized structure, with over 200 operating companies across the globe, each of which had its own IT function. But in the late 1990s, senior management recognized that in the IT area considerable savings could be gained by creating a shared IT service. To accomplish this, the IT infrastructure project was launched in 2001 with the goal of optimizing, standardizing, and leveraging the shared service. It was estimated that with the completion of the project, approximately $50 million could be saved over three years. It involved taking a collection of people from very different operating companies, different countries, and different cultural styles, and putting them into a single organization—not only assembling them in a single organization that had its own challenges, but then immediately looking at how costs could be reduced by leveraging across organizations. Oh, and by the way, the person responsible for converting the organization also had to ensure that 110,000 personal computers were upgraded to the newest operating system.

The Infrastructure Optimization project had all the elements of high Virtual Distance: physical distance, operational distance, and affinity distance. The project called for a leader who understood the challenges posed by Virtual Distance. Fortunately for J&J, they had the perfect leader for the project—Karan Sorenson, now the CIO for J&J's Pharmaceutical Research and Development. Not only did Karan manage to complete the project under budget and faster than the original schedule called for, she also saved the company over $200 million over three years—well beyond the estimated target of $50 million.

Karan understood the challenges of Virtual Distance and how to overcome them. More importantly, she had the ability to quickly understand when to lead and when to let others take the helm. Her handling of this project exemplifies ambassadorial leadership in her balancing the concern for both tasks and people. From the outset, Karan had an intuitive understanding of Virtual Distance. Here's an example of Karan's thoughts on leading a virtual team.

From a manager's perspective, to be successful one of the number one things that you have to do is almost bend over backwards to accommodate others in their time zones. Not an issue when you are collocated, but in many cultures it is a sign of respect and feeling valued when the manager stays on your time zone instead of saying, "Okay, I'm here on the East Coast, so I'm going to have a meeting on Friday without worrying about people in the United Kingdom or Asia. You have to make sure you have a balance and understanding of cultural diversity as well as time constraints and the ability to think about others instead of just what you're trying to accomplish.

As we noted earlier, the Infrastructure Optimization project was spread across the globe and actually included 140 different countries. In order to make the project manageable, a core team was formed representing key regions: North America, Latin America, Europe, and Asia. Two representatives from each region were selected by Karan because, as she said:

I had at least two in each region because I didn't want things to become too centric to a particular country. We wanted to avoid, "Everybody in Europe has to do what Belgium wants, and Asia has to do what Singapore wants." There was enough of a spread and balance so that everyone knew that there would be challenging going on.

One of the dangers in structuring a team or organization globally is an imbalance based on location. Too many or too few people in one location can tip the scales and make one group feel like outsiders. Karan deliberately avoided this and also built in protection against "groupthink" or the tendency to go along with the easy decision. She made sure that there would be some constructive arguing over how to best get the job done.

Karan was careful to choose the team not only based on their location and expertise, but also based on what she knew of their social network. A natural boundary spanner herself, she recognized that within each region she needed people who were also able to span the boundaries between locations and organizations.

In addition, during the early stages of the project, Karan also understood the importance of clarity, not only for the team but for herself as well.

> The first thing was to truly understand the goals and objectives, get enough background and data to bring some clarity to what we needed to do. This is difficult enough without having it be ambiguous. We're trying to be very clear, clean, and focused so that people know what they have to do.

The lesson here is that as a leader, *you* have to be clear before you can begin to communicate with your team.

The project actually began with conference calls and follow-up e-mails because things were moving too fast to wait for a big kickoff meeting. Interestingly, none of the team knew one another before the project began, so there was no real relationship history—one of the factors in reducing Virtual Distance. This was quickly overcome, however, beginning with the first face-to-face meeting a few months into the project.

> We brought together everyone that we had identified to be on the team to make sure that we all had a common understanding of what was going on. A big part of it was making it so that it was much more relaxing than the ominous job that we had ahead of us. We actually shared things like our cultural backgrounds, and everybody brought something from their region of the world or country that they thought might be unique about them to share with others. So it became a little bit more of a personal sharing rather than, "Okay, this is what we're going to do, hit the beach, take the town, and get back on the boat for the next fight." It was more about getting together and respecting and appreciating one another. At that point we agreed to start having some group norms so we agreed to begin rotating conference calls so it's not always 2 AM for the guys in Japan. We laid out a tentative schedule that showed everybody being inconvenienced at one point or another.

Openness and respect for different cultures, making time to build relationships and having a little fun all serve to build trust and help people understand one another. There's also an appreciation for time differences and for lowering status differences that might be perceived. Recognizing people for their contributions rather than their position lowers social distance. As Karan said:

> No one group had higher priority than the others. We all had the same kind of work to do. It was equally important for Asia to be successful as it was for the United States, even though the dollars were less in Asia, but at the end of the day, the work was just as hard to do regardless of where you were. One of the jokes—even though nobody wears ties anymore—we'd say, "Leave your ties and titles at the door." So when we came in we were one team. Even though I was leading the team, I behaved as a regular team member as much as possible. Everybody was a contributor, and there was a talent that they had, and people felt proud of what they were good at and volunteered to share.

While everyone's busy and working on multiple projects, we're really not sure what people on the call are doing or whether they're paying attention. This was, of course, true for the J&J project as well. Karan sometimes used video as a tactical tool.

> But we would have it every so often just because you felt like you had to get another sense involved in the conversations. In the audio conferences, you could tell that people were some-times distracted and you figured they had their speakerphone on mute, they were listening and they were working on their e-mail, or somebody from the office was talking to them. You could tell that there were fcertain levels of engagement that started to drop off over time. It's not easy to keep people fully engaged when they only have limited senses that they can bring into the meeting. Every now and then I would announce, "Let's have a videoconference." It was interesting. The biggest plus was not the meeting itself but the ability at the beginning of the meet-ing to wave at each other and make some kind of connection. You could smile and wave, "Hey how are you doing?" and then

you could get into the meeting stuff, but that little connection is almost like a little charge of electricity to help close a little bit of the gap. It doesn't completely do it, but it helps. They never knew when I would call it. I would just say, "Hey, it's time for a videoconference—I want you guys to see that I lost weight." And then they would all laugh. It helps to make a little bit more of the connection.

One of the other things we did, which is simple, but when we did a lot of the audio conferencing everyone sent their pictures and we printed out everyone's picture and set them by the phone. You would catch yourself looking at the picture of the person who was talking on the phone. I noticed that by doing something that simple, they tended to connect a little bit better than just talking at air. It gave everyone a point of focus. Maybe, from a communications perspective, people want to have a focus to connect to. Even something as silly as that was very useful. People would say, "I'm looking at you right now." I'm shaking my hand at you, you get me? And everybody would start laughing. People were pretty skeptical at first, but they got into it. One day we had a meeting where people weren't in their regular location, and they got upset they didn't have the pictures.

So video was used to make sure people were engaged, and the pictures were used as a way of keeping the emotional connection with the other team members. The emotional connection between these previously unacquainted folks became so strong that Karan says that when they'd get together, it was more like a family than a project team. This connection, along with everyone's taking a leadership role, led to some great examples of organizational citizenship.

Part of building a team is creating a sense of accomplishment, a sense of accountability, and not wanting to let down the other members of the team. What was really nice was actually seeing our guys from Asia, who were phenomenal at rolling things out, because they are so used to doing everything with absolutely nothing at all, they volunteered to go to Europe to help with the rollout in Europe. That was not something that we asked; instead, it was "We're struggling in Europe, we're getting resistance, it's

August, a lot of people are on holiday here; we don't know how we're going to make the timelines." So people from the other areas said, "I've got some things that I've done that might be helpful," and they would pull off a sidebar conversation and share lessons learned, best practices, and it was great to see members of the team say, "If you want, I'll send some of my best folks out there to help you". Everybody was playing for the team not just their piece of it.

Finally, Karan led by stepping up as an advocate for her team when it was necessary. She describes it this way,

> Even though I was leading the team, I behaved as a regular team member as much as possible. But, of course, when issues would come up, I would step into my leadership role to take on the ugly job of dealing with politics or bully-type behavior. They used to kid me and say, "You get all the ugly jobs," so I'd say, "That's why they made me the boss."

In addition, Karan argued (and won) with senior management that her team should be measured on a specific set of metrics and rewarded based on how they did against them. They all ended up getting 120 percent bonuses.

One of the ways that Karan dealt with differences in cultural values and communication styles was to confront them early and get them out in the open.

> I spent a lot of time talking individually with people to get the rules of engagement straight. One of the things that helped with cultural diversity was recognition and acknowledgment of different communication styles. We all shared what our preferred style was. Some people preferred doing everything in e-mail because they liked to spend a lot of time thinking about it, having a chance to get it the way they wanted it so they could get the message clearly across. So some people were very adept at writing and liked to use e-mail. But then there were others who were much more verbal and interactive. I tell my people, "Hey, guys, I'm a voice person. If you need me or want to get something to me, leave me a voice mail. A lot of times, I'll get a voice mail saying, "Karan, check your e-mail." What we did was to let everybody

know what their preferred style was so we could respect that and consider that."

We would argue that Karan Sorenson is not just an example of someone who did a good job on a big project, but more than that. She represents the characteristics that will be needed to lead effectively as businesses continue to become more distributed, more global, and more networked. We're not alone in recognizing that traditional views of leadership need to be rethought. Warren Bennis, one of the most acclaimed experts on the subject of leadership, recently wrote the following:

> The study of leadership will be increasingly collaborative because it is precisely the kind of complex problem—like the genome—that can only be solved by many fine minds working together. Leadership itself is likely to become increasingly collaborative. We already have a few examples in the corporate world of successful power sharing— the triumvirate at the top of the search engine Google is a good example. And other shared-power models will surely develop as the most creative organizations deal with the issue of leading groups in which the ostensible leader is neither more gifted nor less gifted than the led[2].

SOME FINAL THOUGHTS

If you are leading or going to lead a team similar to the one that Karan led or almost any team that is distributed, here are some questions you can ask yourself:

Clarity in Communication

- ☐ Do I truly and completely understand what needs to be done to be successful?
- ☐ Have I communicated this vision clearly? Am I sure that everyone understands it?

- ☐ On a day-to-day basis, do I use various modes of communication to their best effect?
- ☐ Do I appreciate and respect others' style of communication?

Cultural Sensitivity

- ☐ Have I been open to learning and appreciating the differences in cultural values and styles of the members of my team?
- ☐ Have I taken steps to share cultural values and styles of communication among all members of the team?

Context Sensitivity

- ☐ Do I understand the context in which people live and work?
- ☐ Do I have a good sense of how the individuals in this group think when they're on their own and in a group?
- ☐ Do all members share a common view, and, if not, what can I do to help them form a similar point of view?

Boundary spanning activities

- ☐ Have I taken steps to build relationships between members of the team from different geographic areas, organizations, and disciplines?
- ☐ Do I set norms that allow team members to share the load when it comes to being inconvenienced because of time zones, travel, and other issues related to distance?

☐ Have I helped build relationships between my team and other people or organizations essential to the project?

☐ Do I manage the balance between face-to-face, video, and other modes of communication so that relationships are strengthened and maintained?

Advocacy

☐ Do I represent my team effectively to senior management or other important stakeholders?

☐ Do I make sure that the team is appropriately recognized and celebrated for their accomplishments?

☐ Do I make sure that the team is properly rewarded?

Shared Leadership

☐ Have I set expectations that allow all team members to take a leadership role?

☐ Are team members respected by one another for their contributions rather than their position?

☐ Am I able to lead less when it is appropriate and take the lead when it is appropriate?

☐ Have I identified the right people to take the lead for different tasks?

Leader Intent

☐ Have I communicated all I need to with the attachés about the purpose and possible ways forward with this project?

☐ Have I allowed the attachés enough input into the process so that they feel their views are well represented?

☐ Have I been able to reach an agreed-upon understanding of how to move forward that satisfies the
mission and also helps the attaché to reach his or her
personal goals?

NOTES

1. B. M. Bass, *Transformational Leadership: Industrial, Military, and Educational Impact*, (Mahwah, NJ: Erlbaum, 1998).
2. Warren Bennis. The challenges of leadership in the modern world. *American Psychologist*, 62 (2007): 2–5.

~8~

Re-imagining Innovation

Innovation can include everything from coming up with great new products to new ways of solving business problems. However as we define it, innovation is what allows companies to remain vital and to grow. But what are the implications for innovation when it comes to working virtually? We discuss some of the key issues surrounding innovation and how virtual relationships can be harnessed not only to keep new ideas flowing but to translate those ideas into reality and re-imagine innovation in the globally integrated enterprise.

BRAINWAVES AND MUSICAL CREATIVITY

At the Royal College of Music in London, one might find young musicians lying restfully listening to headphones. Not so unusual, you might think, except what they're listening to is the sound of their own brains. Our brains are constantly producing electrical signals in the form of wave patterns that can be captured by an electroencephalogram (EEG). The patterns vary as our brains become more or less alert or relaxed. High frequencies occur when we are excited or agitated, and low frequencies occur when we are relaxed. Students connected to an EEG can learn how to control the frequency of their brainwaves through audio feedback. The goal is to enter a theta wave state—a state between sleep and wakefulness. The theta state is when a lot of ideas come to us, where our minds are more open and we make connections that our alert brain would filter out. John Gruzelier, a neuropsychologist, hypothesized that such training could improve creative musical performance. He ran a tightly controlled experiment in which half the students underwent the neural feedback program and the other half did not. Their musical performance was then evaluated by experts who did not know which students underwent the treatment. The results were startling. The students who learned to control their theta waves improved a full grade, but there was no change in the control group.[1] Interviews with students who participated in the experiment revealed that one of the reasons that their performance improved was their enhanced creativity in interpreting and playing.

Theta waves may be good for creativity, but when we're awake our brain produces different kinds of waves. When we're concentrating on a task—evaluating ideas, for example—we produce beta waves. This research suggests that in order to be creative, we need to be able to move back and forth between this relaxed, idea generation state and the more alert, evaluative stage.

BRAINSTORMING CREATIVITY

The cognitive science on brain training is in its early stages but these findings agree with the research on creativity and innovation. The idea generation phase, researchers agree, should be clearly separated from the idea evaluation phase. Remove the apprehension about being criticized from idea generation and let the ideas flow freely so that as many ideas as possible can be generated. Brainstorming is an approach that follows this principle. Brainstorming sessions involve having a group generate as many ideas as possible. The ideas are not evaluated but can be built upon or used to trigger other ideas. Brainstorming seemed like a great idea when it was introduced in the 1950s, but researchers studying brainstorming discovered something surprising. Individuals working alone could produce more good ideas than a comparable number of individuals in a brainstorming group.

Study after study shows that the number of ideas produced by individuals working alone will outpace the number produced by the same individuals in a team. In some cases, individuals have been shown to generate twice as many ideas as a comparable number of people in a team. There are a couple of reasons why solo performers do better. One is the apprehension that people might feel about expressing their ideas in a group. Another is that only one person can talk at a time in a group, so in a given amount of time the number of ideas discussed by the group is fewer.

It may be a bit premature to start training everyone to control their brainwaves, but all of the research suggests two conclusions. First, initial idea generation can be done effectively by individuals, and second, physical distance may actually be an advantage since individuals may be more relaxed working alone (closer to the theta wave state) and distance can help to lower the apprehension of criticism. Ideas are not enough to produce innovation, however.

CREATIVITY VERSUS INNOVATION

Creativity and innovation are not the same thing. An idea can be original and creative, but it might have no application. We define innovation as "imaginative activity that is fashioned to produce outcomes that are both original and have creative value."[2]

It is no wonder that innovation is a frequent topic in both the popular press and in academic journals. Organizations rise and fall based on how innovative they are. What typically comes to mind when most people think of innovation are products like digital cameras, the iPod, or cellular phones. But innovation can take many forms, including services, processes, and even ways of structuring and managing organizations. The virtual, networked organization is such an example, as is the virtual team. But as we have seen, working virtually is different than working face to face, and managing those differences effectively is critical for the survival of organizations and economies.

A lot of our own work has related to innovation in one way or another, and we think it's safe to say that nobody has yet figured out how to best harness the power of the Internet to improve our innovation capability. There are some things that we might be able to do better and other things that we have not figured out how to do as well when we are working together virtually.

INNOVATION AND GOLF BALLS

Based on our definition, in order for an idea to become a true innovation, it must have two characteristics: originality and utility. Ideas can develop in a lot of different ways, and in many cases the process is far from systematic. In fact, in the new product development arena, the generation of new ideas is often referred to as the "fuzzy front end" because it is not really clear how it occurs or what the best process is. Idea generation has been referred to as experimental and often chaotic,[3] which might explain how a DuPont chemist ended up being named as one of golf's 35 most influential people by *Golf Digest*. In the early 1960s, Richard Rees was doing laboratory research on polymers and unexpectedly discovered an unusual gel. It was as clear as glass and unusually tough and resilient. Though the applications were not apparent at the time, the substance, trademarked as Surlyn, eventually became the standard coating for golf balls. If you don't play golf, you have encountered Surlyn as the clear packaging wrap for CDs, toys, electronic equipment, and many other products. It took a lot more than an accidental discovery to make Surlyn a commercially successful innovation. In fact, DuPont almost gave up on it several times. But other people at DuPont were able to develop the material for different product applications, and still other people were able to translate those applications into commercial viability.

The Surlyn example occurred well before the Internet, of course, but it illustrates the two broad categories of innovation activity: exploration and exploitation. Like idea generation, Rees's discovery is a good example of the exploration phase of innovation. Finding markets for Surlyn is an example of exploitation. The exploitation of Surlyn was accomplished through the social networks of people in research and development (R&D) and marketing who were able to make the right connections. In a virtual world, it is this social networking aspect of innovation that has to be carefully managed.

SOCIAL NETWORKS AND TACIT KNOWLEDGE

Where do new ideas come from? Some, like Surlyn, are accidental and some come from ideas generated by individuals. But many others arise collaboratively from the interactions and exchanges that we have with people in our social network. Imagine that you are an engineer working on a difficult problem and you are stuck. You wander down the hall (not too far, as we have learned from Allen's research on distance) and talk to Jill about the problem. Jill doesn't have the answer but she knows someone else who might be able to help—a colleague named Udo, whom she met at a conference in Germany. You e-mail Udo and set up a conference call, and after listening to your problem, he is able to provide an idea of how the problem might be solved by referring you to an article that he just read. This scenario is a common one. Innovations do not occur in a vacuum and usually involve input from more than one or two people. Social network analysts would refer to Jill as a close tie and to Udo as an indirect tie. Also, Jill is a boundary spanner because she spans the boundary between your organization and Udo's (see Figure 8.1). In our own research, we found that innovation in projects was strongly related to having indirect or weak ties through different members of the team. Social network researchers have found that it is the indirect or weak ties that provide new information. The people with whom you have close ties generally know pretty much everything that you know, but the weak ties— people you know indirectly through someone else or know

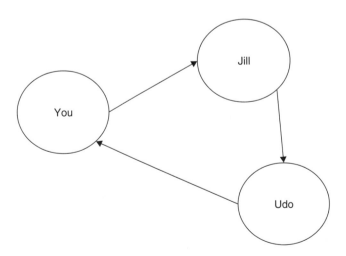

FIGURE 8.1 Social Networks and Innovation

only casually—are likely to have different information. This different information is often the key that enables you to solve a problem or come up with a new approach. In the case of Udo's tip, the information took the form of explicit knowledge—knowledge that is written or archived and can be accessed by anyone. The Internet works pretty well for explicit knowledge; in fact, it has opened up a huge repository of information that is accessible to anyone, assuming they know where to look. Electronic libraries, Internet search engines like Google, list serves, and many other tools are readily available and getting better all the time.

Virtual distance is less of a problem when the need is to share explicit knowledge. But there is another kind of knowledge called tacit knowledge. Tacit knowledge is a bit hard to define but it might be thought of as "know-how." It's what people know that has not been formally expressed or written down. Tacit knowledge can be critical for making breakthroughs in innovation since it represents something that is not generally known to most people. Because it is exchanged person to person, virtual distance can play a big role in the exchange of tacit knowledge. A good example is in the field of laser technology. In the late 1990s, scientists in the United States and the United Kingdom were working on improving laser devices by using sapphire crystals. A major impediment to the use of sapphire in lasers was the difficulty of measuring its quality or Qfactor, a critical property for laser devices. A team working in Glasgow had great difficulty in solving this problem, but it turned out that Russian scientists claimed to have solved the problem 20 years earlier.

It is no surprise that the U.K. scientists' trust in the Russian claim (and the Russian scientists) was low. Physical distance and affinity distance were particularly high between the two groups. This all changed when one of the Russian scientists was invited to Glasgow and was able to share some of the tacit knowledge that he had with the U.K. group.

The visit helped to reduce virtual distance. Physical distance was eliminated, and relationships were developed, which reduced affinity distance. This allowed trust to increase and the tacit knowledge needed to advance the technology was transferred.[4]

The laser story is another example of the importance of weak ties. Bringing together people who have weak ties has worked in many other contexts because it is more likely that new ideas will be exchanged. The research on teams shows that diversity, particularly functional diversity, results in more innovation. Getting people together from different disciplines leads to more breakthrough ideas.[5] For example, Xerox Corporation's Palo Alto Research Center brought together a widely diverse group of natural, social, and computer scientists which led to major innovations in personal computing. At the anecdotal level, a major pharmaceutical company, for economic reasons, deviated from its practice of locating scientists from different disciplines in different buildings. They were forced to house scientists from chemistry, biology, and other sciences in a single building in Montreal. The location in Montreal made possible multidisciplinary interchanges and allowed different perspectives and ideas to flow, resulting in the Montreal facility's becoming the most productive R&D lab in the company.

CASE STUDY: THE HUB

GlaxoSmithKline, like most companies, has multiple teams working on different kinds of innovation. Also, like most multinational companies, employees were distributed all over the globe, and in many cases this meant virtual interactions with many of the attendant issues that we have discussed throughout this book. In 2006, GSK took an interesting approach to decreasing the virtual distance within its product development teams. They decided to collocate team members. GSK went a step beyond just collocation and initiated the hub concept. A hub is a large room with no internal walls and something that looks like a big kitchen table in the middle. If you work in a hub, you are probably one of about 30 team members. You have to find a desk when you come in—all seating is open. You have a portable phone and a portable filing cabinet. If you need privacy for a conference or some quiet time, there are separate rooms on the periphery that you can work in. The kinds of products that GSK develops—dental care, for example—require a variety of functional expertise, including regulatory, medical, marketing, and R&D—exactly the kind of cross-disciplinary mix that is ideal for generating new ideas.

Bringing these folks together lowered virtual distance. Physical distance was eliminated. Operational distance became a nonfactor, and affinity distance was lowered through relationship building and the efforts of GSK staff to prepare employees for the transition to this very different style of working. For instance, they use the Meyers-Briggs Type Indicator and other measures to facilitate the interactions and relationship building between team members.

Does the hub work? It's a bit early to tell for sure, but indications are that more good new ideas are being generated for the pipeline of new products and that people are collaborating more effectively. In fact, GSK has invested in five hubs in its New Jersey location and a number of additional hubs in the United Kingdom.

THE WEB

Bringing people with different ideas together is great if you can manage it, but organizations are increasingly geographically dispersed, so how do we get new ideas when people are not collocated? One way is to harness the web for idea generation. IBM has been a consistent leader in innovation and is usually at the top in objective measures such as patents. But Nick D'Onofrio, the executive vice president for innovation and technology, expresses a broader view of innovation when he says, "In the 20th century, at IBM, we were all about engineering and technology. But now, we define innovation differently. We tell our employees, 'You may not be an inventor or a discoverer, but you will be an innovator.'"[6] IBM's Think Place is a web site open to all IBM employees. You can submit an idea on anything. Once an idea is submitted, it is reviewed by a panel of experts and evaluated. If it is accepted into the system, it is posted, and other employees can comment on or suggest improvements to the ideas. Employees who submit ideas that are accepted receive cash bonuses. In November 2006, IBM announced that it would invest $100 million in the 10 best ideas submitted.

New ideas can also be generated through online forums. QWAQ is an example of a sophisticated online forum that is being used by several companies to foster collaborative innovation. QWAQ includes some unique features such as avatars and a simulated laser pointer that allows users to easily see what other people are looking at and what they are working on. Social Presence is increased through Voice-over Internet Protocol (VoIP) and instant messaging. QWAQ also allows users to save the contents of the forum at any time.

Another form of innovation that works well on the Internet is open source. Open source, or free revealing, is unlikely to generate breakthrough ideas, but it is effective for incremental improvements. This has been a feature of software development for some time. Using the Internet, thousands of individuals contribute to open source software projects. The Linux Operating System and the Apache Web Server are examples of software that has been consistently improved by users. But open source is not used just for software. Eric Von Hippel, in his book *Democratizing Innovation,*[7] gives several examples of products and technologies that were improved significantly after the manufacturers decided to freely reveal the design or process details that are usually kept secret. Medical equipment, lithography, and sports equipment are a few examples.

VIRTUAL DISTANCE AND INNOVATION

We have discussed some of the ways that innovative ideas can be developed, but taking those ideas and creating commercial value involves a different set of activities. In some cases, the cycle time for an innovation to achieve its commercial value can be quite long. Fiber-optic cable is an example of a technology that was available for many years before it was implemented in the market. The cycle time for many other innovations is quite short. Incremental improvements, such as Microsoft's latest version of its Zune MP3 player, were implemented in about a year. Regardless of the cycle time, though, the activities involved in exploiting an innovation (i.e., creating commercial value) are similar. We identify six major activities:

1. Managing the front-end of innovation
2. Creating a clear and consistent vision
3. Effective collaboration
4. Effective processes
5. Senior management support
6. Effective information exchange[8]

As organizations become more distributed and networked, virtual distance will play a bigger role in innovation. Figure 8.2 shows the innovation activities related to both exploration and exploitation and suggestions as to how each type of virtual distance can be managed.

FIGURE 8.2 Overcoming Virtual Distance for Innovation

Innovation Activity	Physical Distance	Operational Distance	Affinity Distance
		Exploration	
Front end: brainstorming	Not a barrier	User friendly sites like Think Pad	Values and language may be important
Front end: collaborative idea generation	Face-to-face meetings can facilitate tacit knowledge exchange	Open source innovation; web-based forums (QWAQ)	Face-to-face meetings can facilitate the development of trust
		Exploitation	
Clarity of vision	Periodic face-to-face meetings	Managing video– and audio conferencing effectively	Ambassadorial leadership
Teamwork	Periodic face-to-face meetings	Use audio/video to increase presence and e-mails to exchange data and information	Ambassadorial leadership; prior relationships; trust development
Process	Face-to-face meetings at outset and end of phase	Project management tools; design software	Development of a shared mental model
Senior management support	Face-to-face meetings	Audio/videoconferencing	Ambassadorial leadership
Information exchange	Capturing and recording of information in archives	Audio/videoconferencing; forums	Shared leadership; prior relationships and development of trust

154

The Front End

Brainstorming   In general, virtual distance is less of a problem for brainstorming. Physical distance may actually be an advantage for some brainstorming-type idea generation. Being separated from other people allows the individual to be more relaxed, less apprehensive about negative feedback, and freer to express original ideas. Operational distance can be managed with user-friendly sites like IBM's Think Place. Make it easy and convenient to use and people can submit ideas whenever they get one. Affinity distance is less of a barrier also, though common values and language are important. Shared values ensure that ideas are in sync with the organization's culture, and language is important to clearly communicate the idea.

Collaborative Idea Generation   Virtual Distance creates some challenges for collaborative idea generation. Physical distance creates a barrier for tacit knowledge exchange and may be insurmountable unless face-to-face meetings can be arranged. Operational distance can be countered through the use of open source innovation and web-based forums, such as QWAQ. Affinity distance can be lowered through prior relationships, shared values, and face-to-face meetings. This will also raise the level of trust needed for successful collaborative idea generation.

Clarity of Vision

Once an idea has been defined, creating a clear vision allows everyone on the team to have a common understanding of what is being developed, what needs to be done, and what they have to do to get there. The vision has to be communicated and periodically checked to make sure that all team members continue to have the same understanding. This allows a shared mental model to be developed which enables teams to function together seamlessly. The essential pieces of the vision should also be consistent. The NASA Orbital Boom Sensor System project that we discussed earlier had a clear and simple vision: "Develop a capability for inspecting damage to the Orbiter Thermal Protection System while in orbit by the launch date." Although details of the system changed over time, the essential vision remained the same throughout the project and allowed the team to share a common mental model of what they were developing. Physical distance is a challenge for communicating a clear and consistent vision. Getting people together creates excitement and enthusiasm and can help people accept and internalize the vision, so face-to-face meetings at the outset of a project and at critical junctures are highly desirable. Operational distance can be managed by the effective use of video- and audio conferences and other Internet tools such as e-mails where appropriate. Affinity distance can be managed by using some of the principles of ambassadorial leadership to ensure that everyone has a common understanding of the vision.

EFFECTIVE COLLABORATION

Creating commercial value from an innovation is typically a multidisciplinary affair. It requires bringing together people with different backgrounds and different points of view. GlaxoSmithKline's hub is one way to facilitate effective collaboration when multiple disciplines are involved. Teamwork also involves trust, culture, and many of the other factors discussed extensively elsewhere in this book. Physical distance can make effective teamwork challenging. Periodic face-to-face meetings can help build relationships and trust between team members. Operational distance can be managed by the effective use of video- and audio conferencing. Allow time for social exchanges; make sure that all team members can participate and that everyone has an appreciation for everyone else's context. Affinity distance can be lowered through ambassadorial leadership, especially the boundary-spanning and shared leadership aspects. For critical projects, team members with prior relationships can be selected to ensure higher levels of intrateam trust.

PROCESS

Process can mean a formal approach, such as the StageGate Process[9] or formal processes used in software development, or something much less formal. Regardless of the process used, it should have several characteristics. First, it should have multiple phases, and all of the phases should be understood by everyone on the team. Second, the standards or criteria for success at each stage should be clear and unequivocal. Third, the decisions as to what to do after each stage should also be clear. Do we proceed to the next phase? Recycle? Stop the project? Finally, everyone needs to have a common understanding of the process and follow it. Physical distance can be lowered by periodic face-to-face meetings, which can be used to review the process, evaluate each phase, and make decisions. Operational distance during the phases can be managed by using audio or video when necessary, as well as web-based design tools, document sharing, and other software. Affinity distance can be managed by the development of a shared mental model through the same activities that develop effective teamwork.

SENIOR MANAGEMENT INVOLVEMENT

Effective exploitation of innovation means that the leaders must pay attention and get involved. This doesn't mean interfering, but rather making sure that resources are available, barriers are removed, and the team and the team leader are empowered so that decisions can be made quickly and leadership can be shared. Senior management involvement should include face-to-face meetings with the entire project team and periodically with members in different geographic locations. Audio and videoconferencing with the team leader and selected team members can lower operational distance and ensure that the team has resources and is empowered to make decisions. Finally, senior managers can use the principles of ambassadorial leadership to lower affinity distance between themselves and the team.

INFORMATION EXCHANGE

Exchanging information in the exploitation phase means periodically reviewing what was done so that all team members know what everyone has done and plans to do. This allows a shared mental model to be maintained and keeps the team on track. Physical distance is less of a barrier for exchanging explicit information in documents and archives, for example. For exchanging tacit information, face-to-face meetings may be necessary. Operational distance can be managed with audio and videoconferencing and the use of forums. Finally, shared leadership and prior relationships can help lower affinity distance and increase the trust necessary to freely exchange information.

NOTES

1. T. Egner and J. H. Gruzelier, Ecological validity of neurofeedback: Modulation of slow wave EEG enhances musical performance. *NeuroReport,* 14(2003): 1225–28.

2. This definition comes from a working group of the Institute for Innovation and Information Productivity. (http://www.iii-p.org/).

3. Peter Koen, The fuzzy front-end for incremental, breakthrough and platform products and services (working paper, Consortium for Corporate Entrepreneurship. 2005).

4. Harry Collins, Tacit knowledge, trust and the Q of sapphire (working papers series, paper 1, Cardiff University, Cardiff, UK, 2000).

5. Lee Fleming, Breakthroughs and the "Long Tail" of Innovation. *MIT Sloan Management Review,* 49 (2006): 68–74.

6. Steve Hamm, Thinking the future with IBM. *BusinessWeek,* March 9, 2006.

7. Eric von Hippel, *Democratizing Innovation* (Cambridge, MA: MIT Press, 2005).

8. Gary Lynn and Richard Reilly, *Blockbusters: The Five Keys to Developing Great New Products* (New York: HarperCollins, 2002).

9. Robert Cooper and Elko Kleinschmidt, An investigation into the new product process: Steps, deficiencies and impact. *Journal of Product Innovation Management,* 3 (1988): 71–85.

— 9 —

Technology: The Elephant
in the Room

So far, we've talked a lot about how human qualities and work conditions create Virtual Distance. You may be wondering at this point about Virtual Distance and its relationship to the elephant in the room—technology. We include both hardware and software in our use of the word *technology*, and it's what makes virtual work possible. It's an understatement to say that virtual work has increased rapidly. It's projected, for example, that the percentage of virtual workers in the United States alone will rise to over 15% in urban areas in just a few years.[1] New hardware and software solutions have facilitated this change and continue to be developed at a staggering pace. By the time this book is in print, there will undoubtedly be more new products available to connect us with one another. Trying to make sense of all this is a difficult proposition, but by using Virtual Distance concepts, we can provide a framework for thinking about which solutions may be right for any given set of circumstances and when they can be used most effectively.

The key to working together effectively, of course, is communication. The Internet, phone, and audio and videoconferencing have created a diverse set of tools that can be used to facilitate communications and collaborations

161

across distances ranging from thousands of miles to a few meters. How and when we use these tools, however, depends on a number of different factors, but two of the most important are what psychologists call social presence and media richness.

Social presence is the extent to which a communication medium supports a feeling of presence and a sense that those involved are jointly interacting. In a group setting, it involves feeling like you're present or "in the moment" with other group members and able to interact freely. Media richness is closely related to social presence and includes several different characteristics. Media are considered "rich" when:

- We have the ability to use natural language rather than symbolic information.
- We have a lot of paralinguistic cues such as tone of voice, facial expressions, and gestures.
- We have the ability to personalize information.
- We can get rapid feedback.

We can place various modes of communication on a continuum of social presence and media richness, as shown in Figure 9.1.

At one end is face-to-face communication, which has maximum social presence and richness. We have all of the visual and paralinguistic cues at our disposal to get our message across and make sure that we understand each other. At the other end is Morse code, a purely symbolic mode of communication with no social cues, limited ability to give or receive feedback, and no visual or audio (except for tapping) information to help interpret the message. We don't use Morse code much anymore (if you're old enough, you might remember the code for SOS, but that's probably all). E-mail, which we all use, is not too far away from Morse code.

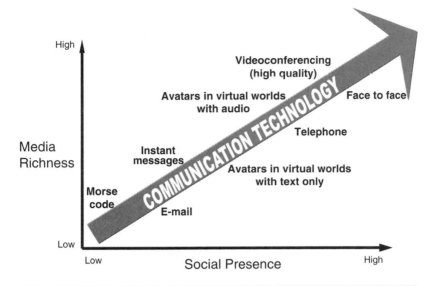

FIGURE 9.1 Communication Technology, Media Richness, and Social Presence

E-mail is, of course, the most widely used mode of communication and has some obvious advantages. It's cheap, quick, and we can use it to convey critical information. For most collaboration within the virtual workforce, it's the most frequently used method of communication.[2] But because e-mail is low in richness and low in presence, it can create some problems. Daniel Goleman recently wrote about his own experience with an e-mail he received from someone he didn't know very well.

> I had met her just once, at a meeting. We were having an email exchange about some crucial detail involving publishing rights, which I thought was being worked out well. Then she wrote 'It's difficult to have this conversation by email. I sound strident and you sound exasperated.'"[3]

Goleman is no slouch when it comes to understanding communication and the emotions that it can arouse. After all, he literally wrote the book on emotional intelligence.[4] But even Goleman was puzzled by the e-mail. He was able to clear things up with a phone call—a richer medium that allows more social presence. Goleman notes that e-mail, because it's devoid of the paralinguistic cues that can convey emotion, carries risks that the message can be misinterpreted. One reason that e-mails are misinterpreted is because we overestimate our ability to convey meaning in our e-mail messages. This is called the egotistic bias. We tend to imagine that other people see and interpret things the same way that we do. This is particularly true when we're communicating via e-mail and lack any social or visual cues to tell us otherwise.

If we think about interacting face to face, there are a lot of different ways that we express ourselves. We use the spoken word—how we say something can give a different meaning: "She killed the man with the knife" is ambiguous as written. Did she kill a man who had a knife? Or did she use a knife to kill a man? A different tone, different emphasis, and even pronunciation can dramatically change the meaning of the same word or sentence from sincere to sarcastic. We also use gestures, alter body position, change our facial expression, and observe the reaction and behavior of the receiver of our communication, which tends to make us adjust our own conveyance.

Herbert Clark and Susan Brennan conduct research on communication. They view communication in terms of what they call grounding: the process by which two people who are communicating achieve a shared sense of understanding as well as a shared sense of participation in the conversation. As they put it, grounding allows both the speaker and the listener to mutually believe that they've understood what the speaker meant. In face-to-face communication, there are six tools for grounding, [5] and we've listed them here:

1. *Copresence,* which allows each party to be in the same surroundings and see what the other is looking at

2. *Visibility,* which allows each party to see the other
3. *Audibility,* which allows each party to hear timing of speech and intonation
4. *Cotemporality,* where each party receives an utterance just as it is produced
5. *Simultaneity,* where both parties can send and receive messages at once
6. *Sequentiality,* where turn taking cannot get out of sequence

The notion of grounding is important because our most extensive communication technology, e-mail, has none of these characteristics, and yet they're the most important when it comes to meaningful communication. When we get an e-mail, we can't know where the other person is. They might be in an office, at an airport, or on the golf course. We can't see them and we can't hear the tone of their voice or inflection of their speech. Are they angry, trying to be funny or serious? We simply cannot know.

In addition, since e-mail is asynchronous, we may get a reply back days after we send a message, thereby creating holes in the last three elements of grounding. Although instant messaging allows something close to simultaneity, e-mail doesn't. Finally, we can and often do get our messages out of sequence. I might schedule a meeting for 2:00 PM on Tuesday and then later read a message that tells me Karen can't make it at that time. Figure 9.2 shows the features of various types of virtual communication.

However, e-mail has a couple of characteristics that face to face doesn't have: revisability and reviewability, which are characteristic of all written communication. Revisability is sender specific. Before an e-mail is sent, it can be edited, reworded, or otherwise carefully crafted. We can write a draft and then decide that we need to explain a point a bit more and add some detail to our message. This might be especially

FIGURE 9.2   Features of Virtual Communication Modes

Characteristic	E-mail	IM	Audio Conferencing	Video Conferencing	Face-to-Face
Copresence					✓
Visibility				✓	✓
Audibility			✓	✓	✓
Cotemporality		✓	✓	✓	✓
Simultaneity		✓	✓	✓	✓
Sequentiality		✓	✓	✓	✓
Reviewability	✓	✓			
Revisability	✓				

important if the message treads on a legal issue. Reviewability is reader specific and is the ability to read over, or review the message as often as we desire. Revisability and reviewability are positive features of e-mail for the most part. We can be careful about what we say and how we say it before we send a message, and when we get a message we can read it or reread it to make sure we understand important details such as the time and place of a meeting. But these same positive attributes might lead to anger and resentment on the part of a receiver. A mildly insulting e-mail might be perceived as highly unjustified because the receiver knows that the sender had time to reword the message, and the receiver can read the message over and over getting angrier each time. E-mail can escalate a conflict because of the lack or delay of feedback and social cues. The reviewable feature of e-mail may produce an obsessive focus on the message, and the revisable feature can allow marshalling of information that can be perceived as overly aggressive.[6] The harshness of the e-mail from Cindy to Jane described in Figure 9.3 looks very different than the transcript of the face-to-face

FIGURE 9.3 E-mail versus Face-to-face Dialogue and Interpretation

The E-mail Version	Transcript of Face-To-Face Meeting
Cindy,	**Jane:** Hi, Cindy. There are a couple of things that I thought we should discuss.
We have to discuss your performance on the Kappa project. Here are just a few of the problems.	**Cindy:** Okay.
You were late to the last three meetings. Your last deliverable was also two days late.	**Jane:** I noticed that you couldn't make the last three meetings on time and was wondering if there is a problem.
When the customer tried to contact you last Thursday you were not in your office and so he called me.	**Cindy:** Well, my daughter has been sick and the babysitter hasn't been able to get there in time for me to make an early morning meeting. Sorry about that.
Finally, you still haven't sent the report that you promised.	**Jane:** I'm sorry to hear about your daughter. I hope it's not serious.
All of these things are causing me some concern and I need to speak with you tomorrow.	**Cindy:** No, just the flu. I think she'll be back to school next week.
Please call me.	**Jane:** That's good to hear. I had the same problem last year when my kids were sick.
Jane	I also wanted to ask about the last deliverable.
	Cindy: Well, Fred has asked me for some help with his problem, and looking at the overall schedule, I felt helping him took priority. I should have let you know that it would be a little late.
	Jane: Yeah, that would have helped, but I'm glad you were able to help Fred. I didn't realize that you were involved.
	Cindy: Yeah. Fred and I really work well together.

(*Continued*)

FIGURE 9.3 (Continued)

The E-mail Version	Transcript of Face-To-Face Meeting
	Jane: Fred's a good guy. **Cindy:** Yeah. He's helped me out a few times, too. **Jane:** I wanted to let you know that I got a call from the customer yesterday and he was looking for you. **Cindy:** Yeah, I know. I was over working with Fred and I picked up the call around 4. I spoke to him and everything is cool. **Jane:** Good. The last thing I wanted to mention is the report. **Cindy:** Oh, yeah. The report. It's just about finished. I have been waiting for input from Ed and Susan. I can send you the draft, but you know the pressure that they've been under, and I did not think a day or two would matter. **Jane:** I understand, but at the same time try to let me know ahead of time. **Cindy:** Okay.

conversation. If we add nonverbal and other paralinguistic behavior, it's clear that what appears to be a withering criticism in the e-mail is simply a minor misunderstanding. The e-mail might seriously harm Jane's and Cindy's relationship and increase the Virtual Distance between them. A face-to-face conversation might actually end up strengthening the relationship and decreasing Virtual Distance (see Figure 9.3).

Because it's still relatively new, there's a lot that we don't understand about the impact of communicating with e-mail. With a couple of exceptions, we simply don't have a lot of good research on the topic. We can observe a few things about e-mail, though. For one, e-mail is particularly bad at communicating subtleties like emotion. One survey found that employees had a need to express emotion with e-mail but have a lot of trouble doing so.[7] Another study described an experiment in which each participant was asked to send 10 e-mails to another study participant. The senders were instructed to make half of the e-mails serious and the other half sarcastic. The e-mail senders were highly confident that they could convey sarcasm, but when the receivers were asked to indicate which e-mails were serious and which were sarcastic, their accuracy was little better than 50 percent—in other words, they did no better than chance.[8] The receivers had no idea whether an e-mail was intended to be serious or sarcastic.

Why do we have so much trouble getting people to understand what we mean with e-mail? Remember the egocentric bias mentioned earlier—the one that contributes to many misunderstandings? Well, it's the same issue in the case of sarcasm or any "intent"-oriented message. The judgments we make when communicating with other people are inherently self-centered. When people are asked to imagine the perspective, thoughts, or feelings of someone else, a growing body of evidence suggests that they'll use themselves as an anchor or reference point. It's completely unconscious, but nonetheless, we assume that everyone else sees things the same way as we do. What's humorous or sarcastic to me may be interpreted as serious or insulting to you. When we interact in person, the feedback from facial expressions (e.g., a furrowed brow) can tell us if we've missed the mark or that the other person doesn't "get it." When we send an e-mail, we may never get feedback. If we do, it may only come after some damage has already been done. Even positive e-mails can be misinterpreted. Research shows that people like to get good news live and "in the flesh." Giving good news with e-mail can be interpreted as less caring and sensitive. In effect, the joy or satisfaction one might get from hearing good news is muted when delivered electronically and is perceived as a lack of consideration because of the way in which it was delivered.

Another issue that can create problems with e-mail is the lack of agreed-upon norms, or standards of behavior, among those involved. Can you answer the following questions?

- Are you expected to return e-mails after working hours or on the weekend?
- When is it appropriate to copy or not copy someone on an e-mail?
- What language is or is not appropriate?
- What is the best way to express different emotions?

There are many other examples for which there's no clear normative behavior. Norms are an important part of culture, and cultures can differ by organization as well as by nation. A good example was related to us by an anthropologist who studies virtual behavior. She happened to be in a café in Australia that had wireless access. Like most of us who carry laptops around, she sat down and then proceeded to log on to her e-mail and began answering messages. Not for long, though. A burly Aussie quickly came by and began yelling at her in colorful language about answering her e-mail in the café. Apparently, social norms in this part of Australia don't allow for work-related behavior in places where people go to relax. Who knew?

Perhaps the greatest problem with e-mail is the sheer number of e-mails that we get every hour of every day. Like a river with no end, the e-mails keep flowing and flowing, threatening to drown us all. Just as we're writing this book, a movement is afoot to deem specific days "e-mail free." But this feeling that we're underwater might be in fact a metaphor for our general inability to separate really important messages from those that are less important or completely irrelevant to our work or lives. How many times are you cc'd on something you barely have an interest in? It takes time to read e-mail and more time to respond. For some organizations, it's such a major problem that they've begun employing more technology to get a handle on e-mails. Some use artificial intelligence to interpret messages and decide whether they're important enough to read and answer. Seriosity, a California start-up firm is using the novel idea of applying an economic model to e-mail.[9] Inspired by the virtual economies of online games like World of Warcraft, the software allows users to attach virtual currency called "serios" to their e-mail messages. Everyone starts out with an equal number of serios and can signal an important e-mail by attaching a higher number of serios. Receivers of e-mail have an incentive to read the e-mails with more serios because they can accumulate serios for their own use. It's too early to tell whether users will adopt this economic model or use the artificial intelligence option, but it's clear that we need better ways to manage our e-mail.

AUDIO CONFERENCING

We all know that star-shaped device that sits on the conference table, the Polycom Sound Station. What you may not know is that the Polycom was actually developed because of frustration with the poor quality of videoconferencing in the late 1980s. The developers, Brian Hinman and Jeff Rodman, realized that the benefit of videoconferencing was mostly in the audio, and the poor quality of the video was more distracting than helpful.[10] The Polycom was full duplex, meaning that more than one person could speak at the same time. This quality allows an easier interchange and a closer approximation to a face-to-face interaction. People can exchange social pleasantries, use humor and give immediate feedback. Teleconferences are missing a couple of the characteristics of grounded communication, however: co-presence and visibility. Copresence allows everyone to see what everyone else is seeing. This problem can be reduced to some extent by using computer-based systems that allow everyone to see the same pictures, text, or slides. Audio conferencing doesn't allow visibility, either—the ability to see all of the other people. In Chapter 7, we described how Karan Sorenson mitigated this problem by using pictures of all of the participants. Interestingly, some recent research has shown that seeing faces can create physiological changes related to arousal.[11] Arousal is particularly important because it means that we're paying attention and are likely to be more engaged. Figure 9.4 gives us an example of how audio can play a role.

FIGURE 9.4   Unintended Consequences of Video Conferencing

In 1979, I was invited to make a presentation describing work I was doing on physical abilities testing for AT&T. Not only did this work have implications for reducing accidents, but we included a study of female employees in traditionally all-male jobs, so there was quite a bit of interest in our research. The presentation was made to the Human Factors Society, and as an experiment, I was asked to use a new videoconferencing system being promoted by AT&T.

I made my presentation to a group of about 50 people in New York City with a link to another group of about 50 people at Bell Labs in New Jersey. The setup was state of the art for the time. A large video screen allowed me to see my slides, and another screen allowed me to see what was being projected to the folks in New Jersey. Another interesting feature was voice activation control of the video camera. The idea was that the camera would move and automatically capture whoever was speaking in the transmitting room.

I began to speak, and after about a minute an older fellow in the first row—let's call him Sneezy—blew his nose. When I say he blew his nose, I mean he really honked! Of course, the camera immediately moved to this loud sound. There he was on the big screen finishing his nose blowing and examining what he had produced. I began speaking again, and after about a minute he honked again, his picture appeared, and he once again gazed lovingly into his handkerchief. Unsure of what to do and completely unfamiliar with the technology, I just soldiered on, and like clockwork every two minutes or so, the honking would resume and the camera would shift to the nose blower again. What I did not realize at the time was that the sound was half duplex, meaning that the loudest sound completely overrode any other sound. As a result, the group in New Jersey had a session unlike any other, consisting of mostly video and sound of Sneezy blowing his nose. The feedback from my colleagues can best be described with the phrase, "Hilarity ensued."

Teleconferencing can work well when Virtual Distance is low. When it's high, however, it can present some problems. A Chinese employee on a multinational team sums up the problem this way[12]:

> Sharing technical knowledge is not a very big problem for me. Since we are both doing the same thing, he [the U.S. colleague] will understand me even if I am not using the correct grammar and sentence. But it is really difficult for me to make social conversation with them. I don't know how to make jokes with them. By the way, I am pretty good at it in Chinese. I don't know how to create a relaxed meeting environment. It makes the meeting very dry and boring, which indeed impacts our communication.

Although this person can discuss task details in terms of their technical aspects, it's unlikely that audio conferencing will decrease Virtual Distance between this employee and his distant counterparts. The kind of social conversation and humor that he refers to are what builds relationships and lowers Virtual Distance.

Another problem with audio conferencing is what can be called *absent presence*. Absent presence means that although a person may be on the phone, it doesn't mean that they're psychologically present. The problem of absent presence is exacerbated by all of the Virtual Distance factors, but two of the operational distance issues in particular are amplified. The first is distribution asymmetry. The bigger the group and the more asymmetric the distribution, the less engaged the participants will be. Participants, especially if they're alone and isolated, are more likely to be doing other things, like answering e-mail and not paying attention to the discussion. The second problem is related to multitasking. For example, I can be on a conference call but because I have a deadline on another project, I am likely to be either working on it at the same time that I'm supposed to be listening or I might have to respond to an instant message, or leaving the room to take a call on my cell phone. The participants may not even know that I've left, particularly if the group is a large one. Some web-based systems try to mitigate this problem. They use an icon or a picture to show whether a person is present or absent—but let's face it, they might leave their icon up while they're doing something else.

VIDEOCONFERENCING

Videoconferencing has come a long way from the early systems produced by AT&T in the 1970s. We can now interact with video from our desktops or laptops and even our cell phones. Tom Sansone, CIO for Credit Suisse, commented about video interaction this way[13]:

> You can see at my desk, desktop video. To me that has really improved my ability to manage over great distance. So I have direct reports that are in Asia and Europe, and, frankly, being able to see them on the screen and talk and see body language makes a huge difference in our communication and I also think in our ability to build our relationship versus just being on the phone.

Video is more media rich and allows more social presence than just audio because we can see the facial expression and some nonverbal behavior of the other person. In addition, video adds the grounding characteristic of visibility. Even lower-quality video systems allow us to see the other person. Communication and feedback are immediate, and we can see the other person. How much nonverbal behavior we see depends on the quality of the video, of course. Most videoconferencing tools don't allow much copresence—the ability to see what everyone else is seeing. Recent innovations in videoconferencing technology attempt to solve this problem with a combination of technology and architecture. Hewlett-Packard's Halo System and Cisco's Tele-Presence System are two examples. These systems attempt to achieve all of the characteristics of face-to-face interaction. Life-size high-definition images of all participants are broadcast to the rest who sit in identical rooms regardless of where they happen to be located. The high-definition images allow visibility, and the similarity of the rooms help to create a feeling of copresence. An additional screen can be used to share graphics, documents, or presentations.

These high-tech video solutions are not cheap, however. The basic cost for installing a Halo room on premises is over half a million dollars, [14] and additional monthly costs are required for maintaining a dedicated high-speed connection.

These high-definition systems can make teleconferencing feel pretty close to really being there. Researchers at Stanford and elsewhere are even developing methods of tracking eye movements, a feature called *gaze,* so that participants will be able to "look each other in the eye." No matter how good the technology is, though, the same factors that we've discussed throughout this book still create Virtual Distance. Teleconferences and videoconferences tend to be task focused and are not designed to easily and informally allow for side conversations, humor, or making a point to go to lunch or dinner after the meeting. These are where solid, enduring relationships are developed.

TECHNOLOGY AND VIRTUAL DISTANCE: SOME PRACTICAL IMPLICATIONS

We've discussed different ways that distributed workers communicate through the use of technology. Good communication is at the heart of all productive work. Without effective communication, organizations struggle to get even the most basic, minimal performance out of the workforce. Communication also plays a critical role in other important aspects of work that we've discussed extensively in this book: trust, innovation, and leadership. All three are essential for the survival of any enterprise, and Virtual Distance poses some special challenges that require careful attention to technology selection and use.

The first practice we propose is to revisit whether communication among the virtual workforce is functioning as it should or whether there are problems that need to be solved. For example, at one of our high-tech clients, we found that while the company was eager to participate in online social networks to attract Gen-Ys, the interns already employed said overwhelmingly that social networking sites like the ones being considered were not something they would normally use voluntarily. We often run across this kind of paradox, where technological solutions are assumed to be the right choice when, in fact, people behave such that they would not be the most effective when compared with other choices.

One simple way to see whether there are problems with the use of communication technology is to ask each person to share his or her conception of the vision for any given project. Ask them what they believe to be the goals and objectives, methods, and processes that will be used to achieve the desired outcomes and also how the project goals relate to the broader strategic goals of the organization. You may be surprised to find that some or the entire group does not share your view. If communication technology is working as it was intended, to facilitate better collaboration, then the visions will be pretty much the same. If communication technology is not helping to inspire or support collaboration, then the visions will be different, or, even worse, group members won't even know what the vision is. As we showed in Chapter 3, a vision that's clear and shared by all is enabled by low Virtual Distance.

Another important indicator of communication technology success can be seen when the group enjoys a shared mental model, which means that everyone has a common understanding of the vision, goals, or mission, and everyone knows what everyone else is supposed to do and when and how they're going to do it. Think of a highly effective basketball or soccer team. Everyone understands the game plan, what every player can do, and how they can support and enhance each other's performance.

A shared mental model also implies that everyone on the team is working with the same information about context. And as we discussed in Chapter 2, the lack of a shared context causes great difficulties with communications in virtual space. In addition, geographic and time-dependent differences tend to create a reliance on asynchronous communication technologies, which can produce interactions that are ambiguous or equivocal. This can mean, too, that feedback loops will be elongated, often leading to delays.

Compounding these issues, cultural and social differences have an influence as well. For example, people in China generally reflect a collectivist culture with high social distance, whereas people in the United States generally reflect an individualist culture with very little thought given to rank or affiliation. Among the former, there's usually a reluctance to ask clarifying questions for fear of "losing face," whereas among the latter, there's sometimes no end to the questions asked in any given communication.

One way to approach the issue of selecting the right communication technology is to rethink the three basic building blocks of communications and then apply them to the selection process. The three basic building blocks are context, information exchange, and meaning and interpretation.

Context, as we've discussed, provides the backdrop against which everything else is interpreted. Copresence, a feature of face-to-face communication, can help in developing a shared context. However, in virtual space, a common context doesn't often exist. In fact, when people are physically separated, their physical and environmental context—the temperature, the lighting, the noise levels, and so on, will almost always be different. If there is also a lack of a shared mental model, it's no wonder that miscommunications are a staple of the virtual worker's communication diet. To bridge operational and affinity distance, when in-person meetings are not possible when they're needed most, it's important then to select technologies that help foster a shared sense of attachment. This means that media that are higher in social presence and media richness should be selected.

Information exchange, which is that part of the communication that involves "swapping data," is straightforward only when both parties, the sender and the receiver, can garner usefulness out of that information. Therefore, language differences and a jagged rhythm or cadence in the exchange can often lead to problems. However, if the purpose of the communication is purely to exchange information, then less rich media can and, in fact, should be used. By leveraging low-presence technologies like e-mail, for the purpose of sharing information that's difficult to misunderstand, people save time and a lot of cost by getting directly to the materials and information they need.

Finally, assigning the right meaning and interpretation to any given exchange is really at the heart of reaching a shared understanding. When barriers such as mistrust, ineffective leadership, and noninventiveness enter the mix, combined with difficulties around establishing a common context and developing free-flowing information exchange, achieving a shared understanding and meaningful interaction is almost impossible. Not only does this pose an organizational problem, but it also becomes frustrating and demotivating to the individuals involved. A shared meaning needs to be achieved when there's a great deal at risk. Therefore, this last essential building block of good communications is most important when the stakes are high and a misunderstanding could cost the company a lot of money or worse. This is usually the case when a major problem needs to be solved or when an expected innovation is not developed—for example the discovery of a new drug. Both problems occur in the context of the organizational strategy as well as day-to-day operations. And the communication technology best suited for each depends heavily on the extent to which affinity distance has yet to be resolved. Another important aspect to meaning and interpretation among group members is the role of the leader. Remember that in Chapter 7 we detailed ambassadorial leadership and pointed out that among their many characteristics is that of being context sensitive. So it's important to remember that not only does communication technology selection depend on the extent to which the basic building blocks of communication are working or not within the scope of group behavior, but also the extent to which the leader influences the work.

Other questions to ask yourself as you evaluate technology in light of Virtual Distance are included in Figure 9.5.

FIGURE 9.5 Questions for Assessing Technology Selection

Physical Distance	*Geographic distance:* Does the software promote presence?	Geographic separation is certainly the most direct contributor to a lack of social presence. When group members need to be close but can't, the software should approximate face-to-face interaction as much as possible.
	Temporal distance: Does the software allow smooth asynchronous communication?	Software should allow users to work together asynchronously as smoothly as possible and should also allow users to know when each group member will be available for meetings, phone calls, and instant messages. If the software can also account for some level of presence, like when someone's online, etc., that's also positive.
	Organizational distance: Does the software allow team members to develop a common identity?	Software can help reduce organizational distance by supporting features that can promote the development of a common identity. Virtual worlds are particularly well positioned to help with this problem by allowing users to create designs and group spaces that feel as though they belong to even the most temporary of teams.
Operational Distance	*Distribution asymmetry:* Does the software allow easy division of groups into smaller groups?	Software should allow easy and seamless division of groups into subsets based on functions or tasks. Collabnet and other companies offer capabilities that particularly allow users to separate parts of the same project and then put everything back together in the larger scheme when needed.

	Communications distance: Does the software allow users to express themselves in multiple ways?	Software that allows users to quickly add video and/or audio ad hoc from wherever they're located is likely to become highly advantageous. Even today, built-in webcams are already allowing people to beam themselves to others. Skype and other voice capabilities along with instant video should be added whenever possible.
	Multitasking: Does the software help to minimize multitasking during conferences and meetings?	Software that helps facilitators check for engagement during meetings, like having the ability to poll participants, can help managers and other meeting leaders keep a high priority on the meeting. Some software automatically signals participants at certain junctures to ensure that they're paying attention.
	Readiness distance: Is the software easy to learn and user friendly, and does it require little technical support?	Complex software that requires a high degree of expertise can create Virtual Distance if team members focus on trying to cope with the software rather than attending to the work. Communication software especially should require little technical skill and support and should have a shallow learning curve.
Affinity Distance	*Cultural distance:* Does the software include assessment features?	Software should allow Virtual Distance managers to occasionally be able to assess different communication styles and value systems. Intermittent surveys or artificial intelligence systems can check for and help to signal the need for discussions around differences between individuals with differing cultural backgrounds.

(Continued)

FIGURE 9.5 (Continued)

	Social distance: Does the software help to promote and recognize the contributions of each team member?	Software systems can't erase differences in social status. In fact, software often eliminates the possibility of fully realizing social distance issues, and that's one of software's benefits in certain cases. What's important about software and social distance is that the system be flexible enough to allow everyone rights into the systems they need. Open software that's accessible by all is a key ingredient to mutual contribution.
	Relationship distance: Does the software allow for social and personal exchanges?	At the heart of relationship distance is a lack of a shared social network. And as we've all come to learn, social networking is one of the main attractions of software these days. Companies can amplify the positive effects of social networking and help to minimize relationship distance by implementing internal social networking capabilities.
	Interdependence distance Does the software promote the perception of interdependence?	Interdependence distance occurs when individuals are not clear on how their work fits into the project as a whole. Graphics software should be employed to develop representations of work which clearly reflect interdependence among group members.

In addition to these additional questions, there are also best practices we've developed that address management endeavors as they relate to trust, innovation, and leadership given Virtual Distance and our technologically based workplace. These are included here in Figure 9.6.

FIGURE 9.6 Best Practices for Improving Trust, Innovation, and Leadership Effectiveness

Practice/Tool	Trust	Innovation	Leadership
Developing project or organizational culture	Set expectations around norms and state values that reinforce integrity and create expectations that people will behave in a trustworthy and benevolent manner.	Establish group norms and values that stress openness, innovation and collaborative solutions.	Develop a "super-culture"—one that leaves intact existing culture and builds upon them. Stress empowerment and shared leadership.
Monitoring	Reward helping (organizational citizenship behavior). Monitor relationships and conflict through e-mail threads, virtual meetings, and personal visits.	Set clear goals and timelines and monitor performance through shared leadership and shuttle diplomacy. Ask those involved to self-rate progress and success levels.	Periodically visit face to face to meet with team members and attachés. Monitor performance through shared workspaces, electronic communications, and e-mail threads as well as periodic conversation.
Selection	Select individuals with requisite competencies especially a high propensity to trust others	Select individuals who are personally interested in the project (self-selected) and who are open to new experiences. Look for those that have high levels of self-motivation and a track record of successfully working in virtual innovation teams.	Select leaders with cross-cultural experience or interest and capacity to share power. Leaders should have established informal status among followers as a result of their contributions as well as their formal status in prior assignments.

(*Continued*)

183

FIGURE 9.6 (Continued)

Practice/Tool	Trust	Innovation	Leadership
Recognition	Recognize helping behaviors in virtual forums, through attachés and personal visits.	Recognize and reward new ideas, collaborative problem solving and goal performance.	Leaders recognize team members by reporting successes and other contributions to a wide group, including a broad span of peers as well as senior management. Conduct virtual reward ceremonies. Report to functional manager on employee behavior.
Teleconferences	Use beginning of video/audio conferences for sharing of personal information and relationship building.	Focus on divergent and new ideas during some part of teleconference. If trust has been established, encourage productive dissent in order to surface additional ideas and approaches to innovation process.	Use teleconference to reinforce vision. celebrate successes, and recognize key individuals or subteams.
Project management software	Communicate planning, changes in plans, and resource interdependencies.	Include results of prototypes, test versions, etc.	Use to keep track of task performance with input from attachés.
Develop shared repositories	Encourage team members to share examples of collaborative efforts	Idea generation, idea evaluation, posting of learnings and tacit knowledge exchange	Allow all team members to keep track of progress and see relationship to other tasks and project as a whole.
Team web site	Include professional and personal background, expertise and experience of all team members.	Community of practice information on seminars, books, webinars, etc.	Reinforce vision, recognition and important news.

In summary, the elephant in the room, technology, is the reason this book exists and is the tool that enabled us to become a virtual workforce. Many argue that Virtual Distance has existed throughout history, and in many respects it's true. For example, Jerry MacArthur Hultin, the former undersecretary of the United States Navy, presented a detailed account of how Virtual Distance has been at work in the U.S. Navy for over a century.[15] And he's right. We've worked as physically distributed groups throughout our history. In fact, the notion of "Commander Intent," first developed in the U.S. Navy in order to seed the leader's message among lieutenants that couldn't communicate with one another during wars, led to the notion of "Leader Intent" in the ambassadorial leadership model. However, even given our past, it's recent technology implementation in all aspects of our lives, including both computing power and communication abilities, that's enabled the widespread use of physically distributed people throughout the world on a daily basis and in everyday life—which, of course, at times feels like a battle but is very different in many ways. So, as we increase our use of technology in the workplace and even in our lives, it is critical to keep the notions of social presence and media richness in mind when selecting and implementing communication tools. These concepts and their application to technology will help to minimize Virtual Distance at the technological level. But when all is said and done, Virtual Distance is an inherently human issue—one that needs to be solved by modifying behaviors and personal attention to others. Technology, as powerful as it is, is only a tool—intelligent or not. People are the reason we go to work, socialize, and are motivated to achieve. People are the ultimate source of joy and happiness. So let's turn to our last discussion about the future and take a look at some of the possible ways forward that might be shaped by the influences of Virtual Distance.

NOTES

1. Michelle Conlin, The easiest commute of all, *BusinessWeek* (2005):78.

2. Arjan Raven, Team or community of practice, in *Virtual Teams that Work,* eds. Cristina B. Gibson and Susan G. Cohen (San Francisco: Jossey-Bass, 2004).

3. Daniel Goleman, Preoccupations: Email is easier to write (and to misread), *New York Times,* October 7, 2007.

4. Daniel Goleman, *Emotional Intelligence: Why It Can Matter More than IQ* (New York: Bantam Books, 1996).

5. Herbert Clark and Susan Brennan, Perspectives on Socially Shared Cognition, in *Grounding in Communication,* eds. L. Resnick, J. Levine, and S. Teasley, (Washington, DC: American Psychological Association, 1991).

6. Raymond Friedman and Steven Currall, Conflict escalation: Dispute exacerbating elements of e-mail communications. *Human Relations*, 56: 1325-47.

7. Kristin Byron and David Baldridge, Toward a Model of Nonverbal Cues and Emotion in Email, *Academy of Management Best Paper* (Briarcliff, NY: Academy of Management, 2005).

8. Justin Kruger, Nicholas Epley, Jason Parker, and Zhi-Wen Ng, Egocentrism over email: Can we communicate as well as we think? *Journal of Personality and Social Psychology,* 89 (2005): 925–936.

9. Daniel Terdiman, A Cure for Email Attention Disorder? *CNET News.com*, (February 28, 2007).

10. Gary Lynn and Richard Reilly, *Blockbusters: The Five Keys to Developing Great New Products* (New York: HarperCollins, 2002).

11. Hugo Critchley et al., Activity in the brain predicting differential heart rate responses to emotional facial expressions. *Neuroimage*, 24 (2005): 751-62.

12. Kangning Wei, Sharing knowledge in global virtual teams, in *Virtuality and Virtualization,* eds. K. Crowston, S. Sieber, and E. Wynn, (New York: Springer, 2007).

13. Karen Lojeski, Innovation across borders. *CIO Insight*, December 11, 2006.

14. T. Roberts, Hewlett-Packard unveils high-end teleconferencing. *San Francisco Business Times,* December 12, 2005.

15. Managing Virtual Distance Conference, Anaheim, California, November 14–16, 2007, www.iirusa.com/virtual.

~ 10 ~

The Future

Throughout this book, we've defined Virtual Distance and discussed how it is created. We've also talked about its impact on several important outcomes, including performance, leadership, and innovation. Now we take a look ahead and share some of our thoughts on the potential ways in which the Virtual Distance Model could help us into the future.

To recap, Virtual Distance is a by-product of our technological age, embodying a perceived sense of separateness that's risen as communications have become increasingly technologically based and as dramatic changes in the way we work continue to develop.

Virtual Distance as a phenomenon has emerged in the past decade or so. As it continues to increase, there's also been a human cost accompanying the increasing role that technology plays in our social and workplace interactions. In a recent interview, Michael Dell talked about having to turn off his Blackberry during nonworking hours because his family life was suffering as a result of his always being available, connected, and able to work from a distance. This is another side of virtual work—it's accessible 24 hours a day, seven days a week. So the distinction between work and personal life becomes blurred.

Virtual Distance is rising at a time when technology as well as business models are changing. Some, like those discussed in Chapter 6, have been so rapid and extreme, we've had difficulty adapting fully. As human beings, we can integrate only so much of our work activity into our everyday life before becoming overloaded. When this happens, as we discussed in Chapter 2, a cognitive and emotional distance builds. This kind of Virtual Distance occurs for three reasons:

1. Our values, relationships, social status, and/or level of interdependence are not in harmony (affinity distance).

2. Our ability to handle daily operational challenges like multitasking, and selecting the right communication method for the right kind of message that includes all the right meaning is a strain. Add continual challenges posed by technology, and we can become overtaxed and lose our natural sense of who we are through isolation or a collective blindness that comes from being too shielded from others (operational distance).

3. Our physical locations, time zones, and group affiliations are scattered and remote (physical distance).

As we discussed in Chapter 3, high Virtual Distance can result in diminished capacity to innovate, cooperate, and develop close bonds with others. But with our new understanding of Virtual Distance, we now have the insight and tools needed to collectively work through some of these difficulties. To do so, though, requires an understanding of the extraordinary changes that have taken place in such a compressed time frame. To put these into perspective, we first take a brief look at how, historically, prior communication technology affected society.

CULTURAL TECHNOLOGIES THAT CHANGED THE WORLD

In his book *Five Epochs of Civilization,* William McGaughey categorizes world history, as we know it so far, in terms of five civilizations punctuated by what he calls "cultural technology."[1] He defines cultural technology as a way to "amplify personal experience" and includes five communication technologies that profoundly changed the way in which we live. Each civilization is approximated, and a summary of McGaughey's historical interpretation is shown in Figure 10.1.

FIGURE 10.1 Summary of the "Five Epochs of Civilization"

Civilization (Epoch)	Approximate Dates	Cultural Technology
Civilization I	3000 B.C. to 500 B.C.	Writing—in a primitive from where symbols are used to express whole ideas or words.
Civilization II	500 B.C. to 1450 A.D.	Alphabetic writing—letters were used to create words and words could be phonetically recognized.
Civilization III	1450 A.D. to 1920 A.D.	Printing—an extension of alphabetic writing, it was a way to mass produce copies of texts
Civilization IV	1920 A.D. to 1990 A.D.	Electronic communications— including the radio, phonograph, telephone, video recording, and television.
Civilization V	1990 A.D. to ?	Computers—not only capture, store, and transmit images, but can also break them down, manipulate them, and customize them for any given user who can then interact with that information in a two-way communication.

As you can see from Figure 10.1, McGaughey was careful not to say when the fifth civilization might end—the Computer Epoch (McGaughey uses *civilization* and *epoch* to mean the same thing). However, we became curious to see if there was a relationship between cultural technologies and the time changes between them. So we plotted a chart to test our notion that there may be some clues to take away from McGaughey's work with respect to our future. Our results are shown in Figure 10.2.

This chart shows an interesting pattern, one that echoes other technological advancements mapped against time. In a paper written by Gordon Moore, Intel's cofounder, and published in *Electronics* magazine in April 1965, he posited that the number of transistors that could be put onto a square inch of silicon would double about every 24 months.[2]

It would appear that a similar kind of logarithmic curve is shown with respect to cultural technologies through the ages. For example, 1,950 years, the approximate length of Civilization II, is about one-half that of the 3,500 years of Civilization I. Four hundred seventy years, the length of Civilization III is approximately half the prior difference, and 70 years, the elapsed time of Civilization IV, is approximately half the previous difference as well. If we take this

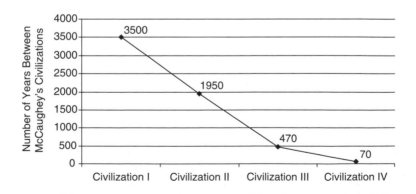

FIGURE 10.2 Chart of McCaughey's Civilizations Over Time

formula to predict how long Civilization V might last, we'd estimate it to be 5 years.

That would take us to 1995, the year in which Netscape, the first commercially available Internet browser, hit a critical mass of almost 100 million people. In fact, many scientists, including economists, use 1995 as a critical cutoff year representing a pre- versus post-Internet economy. Could the World Wide Web and commercial Internet have ushered in Civilization VI? The Internet Epoch, like Civilization III, is punctuated by a new technology that allows us to duplicate as well as manipulate unlimited copies of anything that's been printed, videotaped, or recorded in any way.

Perhaps this is the case. However, if we try and move ahead with this calculation, we soon run out of measurable time. The next Civilization would last less than one year, the next less than one minute, and then nano-seconds and so forth, until time differences, at least the way we understand them as humans, would be imperceptible. The speed of change is, then, increasing so quickly that our ability to adapt and control it is becoming problematic. And if Virtual Distance is high now, what can we expect as technology races forward?

In another parallel, McGaughey's time line, characterized by ever-decreasing rates of decline, also looks similar to a portion of yet another one of Gordon Moore's charts called the "costs and curves" graph. Jon Stokes, in his 2003 paper, "Understanding Moore's Law," reexamined Moore's original work.[3] He highlights the fact that while Moore's prediction of circuits doubling on the same size chip regularly was certainly what he was most famous for, another valuable insight came from his revelation that the costs of developing a highly dense chip would eventually give way to rising defects and other problems that would make integration too expensive. This would require abandoning the original technology at some point in favor of building

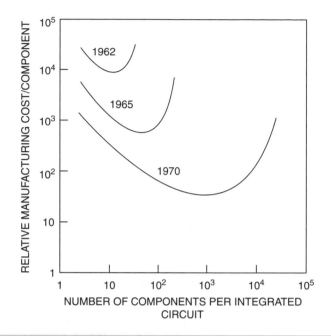

FIGURE 10.3 Costs versus Integration
Source: 2003. Jon Stokes. Understanding Moore's Law, http://
arstechnica.com/articles/paedia/cpu/moore.ars/3.

a better one. Moore's original "costs and curves" graph is presented in Figure 10.3.

According to this chart, while the number of integrated components rises as costs fall in the first part of the curve, eventually, the cost to produce each component begins to rise in the latter half of the curve. Stokes asserts that this is because the number of good chips or "yield" suffers when integration becomes too compressed. Put another way, the complexity is too much for the chip to handle without a lot of costly errors.

A similar curve might be helpful in understanding the potential value of Virtual Distance.

Consider for a moment that there's an analogous curve tracing the costs to maintain or improve human health and welfare, set against our ability to integrate technology and

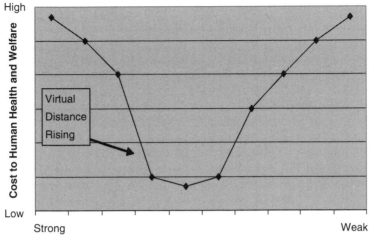

High

Cost to Human Health and Welfare

Virtual
Distance
Rising

Low

Strong   Weak

Ability to Integrate Technology and Information into Work and Life

FIGURE 10.4   Virtual Distance Rising

information into our work and lives. If we were to draw such a curve, it may be that the rise of Virtual Distance is signaling to us that we're approaching a point of diminishing returns. Figure 10.4 shows an example of such a relationship.

As better technology was introduced, the cost of health and welfare fell in many areas. New drugs were discovered that would have been almost impossible to find without the help of highly sophisticated algorithms and uniquely computer-based computations. Our understanding of the human genome and other major scientific breakthroughs were, in fact, possible only because of vast computing power. Results such as the mortality rates of newborns have steadily declined in developed countries and are finding their way into developing countries as well. Average life spans have increased all over the world. In other areas, we are now able to model or simulate certain kinds of problems like the effects of global warming. At Arizona State University, the "Decision Theater" combines visualization, simulation, and cognitive science to examine major policy questions. The work of the Decision Theater has been credited with helping to avoid major environmental disasters by changing plans for major developments.

We've also taken much of the cost out of doing business. True, we still have real estate, offices to keep up, electric bills to pay, and so on; however, relative costs have come down and continue to decline as our ability to use computing power with better, cheaper, and faster communication lines increases. We've also acquired cheaper labor through global arbitrage and taken advantage of a vast pool of international skills and expertise. We are able to more easily and quickly integrate needed information into our work and research, which has led to higher productivity. We can, on a moment's notice, do market research on a new product or find out how the earliest Greek scriptures compare against modern-day orations and quickly discern similarities and differences between us and the ancients.

So, although technology increasingly serves us in many fruitful ways, Virtual Distance is rising due to decreasing levels of physical closeness; problems with day-to-day activities, which often includes an overabundance of technological communications; and decreasing emotional ties developed through affinity building. Just as Elton Mayo discovered that a "human touch" could help productivity rise almost a century ago, Virtual Distance is telling us that a bit of the same might help us even in this highly technological era. In fact, it's likely that lowering Virtual Distance could be the way in which companies avoid higher costs overall into the future.

The Virtual Distance Model clearly shows that getting to highly satisfying work that meets the need for self-actualization and socialization is possible even if we're far apart, working with a lot of technology. To lower Virtual Distance in the future, we need to build Virtual Distance management plans to ensure better integration between our behaviors and our technologies. In the future, to avoid climbing too far up on the latter portion of Moore's cost curve, we need to focus on five critical activities, which we've described for you in this book:

1. Meet, measure, map, and manage Virtual Distance up front.
2. Produce ambassadorial leaders.
3. Reimagine the virtual workforce as virtual ensembles.
4. Look for opportunities to leverage Virtual Distance, as well as minimize it in innovation activities.
5. Select communication technologies based on Virtual Distance profiles.

If we implement this five-step plan, our future will consist of a virtual workforce that's united through lowered Virtual Distance, higher levels of trust and empathy, an increased willingness to help one another, and elevated clarity around vision and goals that are linked where need be, but that also serve individual needs across the network.

And it's not just current management and communication technology that will drive the need to manage Virtual Distance more closely in the future. As we speak, major companies are planning ways to develop 3-D virtual worlds where "universal avatars," virtual facsimiles of ourselves, will be able to roam in and out of any virtual world. The purpose will be to advance work technologies to even further mimic the ways we've worked together in the past. So in cases where Virtual Distance is high between us as "real" people, what might happen when we find ourselves working together as virtual people? It may mean that we'll have no way to know for sure if our colleagues are real or simply computer generated, for example. But if Virtual Distance is not dealt with, then in the very worst of cases, we may begin to lose empathy for one another—empathy derived from trust and a shared sense of purpose. And if this happens, then our working lives would become less satisfying and increasingly sterile.

While that outcome seems extreme, we may in fact be entering into an extraordinary evolutionary shift. Baroness Susan Greenfield, neuroscientist and director of the Royal Academy in London, in her book *Tomorrow's People*,[4] illuminates a possible future full of human beings experiencing life almost completely through a computer-augmented reality. Others, like Edward Tenner, demonstrate how technology creates ever-increasing states of complexity to which we must constantly react and adapt. In his book *Why Things Bite Back*,[5] he describes how seemingly benign advancements can create the need for us to evolve in order to keep up with our own creations.

But in almost all of these futuristic points of view—whether they are scientifically based or even created as fictional works—there's almost always a scenario that features a strong hope that we will "rediscover" our humanity in a way that's positive and moves us ahead as a whole society. In many respects, that's what Mayo discovered almost a century ago when the notion of the mechanistic man was peaking. We believe Virtual Distance can do that for us now.

Virtual Distance gives us a road map that allows us to better understand how we can drift apart and "forget" that we are in fact creatures of emotion and good intent. The Virtual Distance Model helps us to see how we become untethered and provides us a way back to ourselves and each other. By mapping Virtual Distance, we are able to specifically ignite our vision and correct for things that have gone awry. Our ability to assign specific costs to Virtual Distance helps us to measure its direct impact on the bottom line.

Once Virtual Distance effects are quantified, we can rebalance the variables in the distance equation so that they don't become harmful and instead work in our favor. But this will not be easy because it means "abandoning" our prior "fab" (fabrication), as Moore would say, for a newer and better one in terms of management philosophies and technologies. Moore, and later Stokes, argued that once the cost/integration curve inverted, it was time to build something new. And in many respects, people in economics and other global pursuits are reaching that same conclusion with respect to business and economics.

In 2005, economist Stephen Roach wrote that it's time to "give up our time-honored relationships" due to the changed landscape of global information and communication technologies and the effects they're having on world economic models. Neuroscientists like Martin Westwell and Susan Greenfield are focusing their attention on how technologies impact the human brain. Adele Diamond, another researcher, has shown that we need to focus on helping our children at ever-younger ages learn how to develop human relationships without technological mediation. In her award-winning research, she showed that children who were taught to learn how to pay attention to each other in kindergarten and even earlier, went on to lead much more productive and happier lives.

Given this mounting evidence, Virtual Distance—the recognition of it as well as the need to manage it—is becoming more urgent. There is only a short window, perhaps a few years, in which to adjust our course before the next iteration of collaboration technology is implemented on a global scale. We believe that with the discovery of Virtual Distance and the tools we've presented here, we can recognize it, map it, and manage it. New tools can also be developed to help steer our collective ship into a safer harbor and, there, find the next "fab" that will catapult us into a world that's better than the one we live in today.

NOTES

1. William McGaughey, *Five Epochs of Civilization: World History as Emerging in Five Civilizations* (Minneapolis, MN: Thistlerose Publications, 2000).

2. Gordon Moore, Cramming more components on to integrated components, *Electronics* April, 1965.

3. Jon Stokes, Understanding Moore's Law. http://arstechnica.com/articles/paedia/cpu/moore.ars.

4. Susan Greenfield, *Tomorrow's People* (London: Allen Lane, 2003).

5. Edward Tenner, *Why Things Bite Back: Technology and the Revenge of Unintended Consequences*, (New York: Knopf, 1996).

Index

3M Corporation, 57

A
Accenture, 101
Allen, Thomas, 10-11, 148
American Express, 113
Apache Web Server, 152
Arizona State University,
193
Asynchronous
communication 15,
97, 177
AT&T, 172, 174
Aventis, 126

B
Brainstorming, 144-145,
155

C
Chesbrough, Henry, 114
Cisco Systems, 175
Clark, Herbert, 164
Collocation, 59, 63, 66,
125, 151

Credit Suisse, 174
Crick, Francis, 54-55,
57
Critical relationship path,
73, 80-83, 86-87

D
Damasio, Antonio, 18
Dell, Michael, 187
Diamond, Adele, 197
Distance
affinity, 4-5, 27, 33,
41-43, 47-48, 51-52,
58-59, 64, 67, 76-81,
83, 89-90, 102, 104,
126, 129-130, 133,
149-151, 155-158,
178-179, 188
communications 34-37,
41-48, 76-79, 94-96,
99, 102
cultural, 41-43, 48, 76,
94, 97, 102, 129
death of, 9-11, 22
emotional, 10, 23